Baseball's Untold History:
The People

About the Author

A native of Massachusetts and the founder of **Seamheads.com**, Michael Lynch has been a member of SABR since 2004. His first book, *Harry Frazee, Ban Johnson and the Feud That Nearly Destroyed the American League*, was published by McFarland Publishing in 2008 and was named a finalist for the 2009 Larry Ritter Award in addition to being nominated for the Seymour Medal. His second book, *It Ain't So: A Might-Have-Been History of the White Sox in 1919 and Beyond*, was released by McFarland in December 2009. His work also appeared in *Opening Fenway Park in Style: The 1912 Boston Red Sox* and *The Miracle Braves of 1914: Boston's Original Worst-to-First World Series Champions*.

Appearing on the front cover, clockwise from the top: Bill Dahlen, Freddy Parent, Gary Carter, George Sisler, Les Nunamaker, Iron Davis, Don Wilson, and Chris Brown (center).

Baseball's Untold History:
The People

By Michael Lynch

SUMMER
GAME
BOOKS

Portions of this book were published previously online at Seamheads.com

ISBN: 978-1-938545-52-8 (print)
ISBN: 978-1-938545-53-5 (ebook)

For information about permissions, bulk purchases,
or additional distribution, write to
Summer Game Books
P. O. Box 818
South Orange, NJ 07079

or contact the publisher at
www.summergamebooks.com

For my mother, Patricia, who has always believed in me and given me the strength and courage to believe in myself.

Baseball's Untold History Series
by
Michael Lynch

Contents

Part IV – Among the Stars

Part V – Around the Diamond

Quick Hits

Author's Note

The researchers among you will most likely notice a lack of source notes for some of the stories. This is due to a data loss from a computer crash during the preparation of the manuscript. Efforts to reassemble the sources were painfully slow (as well as just painful), and the decision was made to proceed with production, to save the publication schedule as well as my sanity. To fill the information gap, at least partially, a bibliography has been included.

Since **Baseball's Untold History: The People** is only the first of a 4-book series I'll be doing with Summer Game Books, be assured that the upcoming volumes will be fully sourced. Thank you for understanding. I hope you enjoy the book.

Introduction

I've been a baseball fan for as long as I can remember. My grand-father made a scrapbook from newspaper clippings of Babe Ruth's exploits when he was still a star with the Boston Red Sox. My father grew up idolizing Ted Williams, then later, Carl Yastrzemski. I adopted Yaz as my favorite when I was a kid and over the years have been lucky enough to see some all-time greats with my own eyes.

But my true passion lies in the past with men who gave baseball its character; some upstanding citizens, others constantly in their manager's doghouse or on the wrong side of the law. I didn't set out to find these stories, they sort of found *me*. A good friend once joked that I always seem to write about tragic figures—alcoholics, those whose careers were cut short, players who never fulfilled their potential, and some who were just unlucky and died young.

I'm not sure why I gravitate towards those players other than I find them interesting and I sympathize with them. I've finally realized that it's all a bit semi-biographical, that I've dealt with alcoholism, experienced tragedy, mourned the loss of a father who died too young and a sister who was murdered at 34. But I'm also intrigued by the era in which most of these men lived.

It was a time when you could be arrested for "seduction" by promising to marry a woman but not following through. A time when alcohol flowed despite prohibition. A time when shooting at a black man only resulted in a very small fine, or contributing to someone's death came with a small financial penalty. A time when punching umpires was not uncommon but could result in a lifetime suspension.

In the following pages you'll read about the only non-pitcher to commit an error in his only major league fielding opportunity and strike out in his only at-bat. A budding superstar who thought he was going blind, only to learn he had a brain tumor. A star hurler who offered to throw a pennant race, not by throwing games, but by *not* throwing games. A braggart who boasted he could hit .400 against major league pitchers, boxed to a 5-2 record with five knockouts, was once photographed shaking hands with Al Capone prior to a ball game, and went to trial for murder *TWICE* in his life.

Not all of the men in this collection are from a bygone era, though. More modern accounts include a successful pitcher who died of carbon monoxide poisoning under mysterious circumstances; the only man in major league history with at least three hits who batted 1.000 for his career; a hurler who was credited with an official appearance without ever facing a batter; and a former National League All-Star who survived multiple tours as a civilian truck driver in Iraq, but died after being severely burned in a mysterious house fire.

My hope is that this book will appeal to the most hardcore fans all the way to casual observers. It's far less about balls and strikes and hits and outs than it is an attempt to bring these men back to life, back onto the field, and back into the hearts and minds of baseball fans, if only for a moment. I am sure there is no place they would rather be.

PART I

FROM FAME TO MISFORTUNE

The Mysterious and Tragic Death
of Don Wilson

In the spring of 1968, a magazine called *SPORTS STARS OF 1968: BASEBALL* named Houston Astros hurler Don Wilson one of its "Stars of the '70s" based on his rookie season performance in 1967 when he went 10–9 with a 2.79 ERA and tossed a no-hitter at the Atlanta Braves on June 18.[1] At only 22, Wilson seemingly had years of success ahead of him. Little did anyone know he actually had only seven more years of life before it was tragically cut short on January 5, 1975.

Reports of Wilson's death hit everyone hard and left more questions than answers. He had been found dead in his garage, "slumped over a reclining seat on the passenger side of his sports car," the victim of asphyxia due to carbon monoxide poisoning.[2] Apparently he drove into his garage at around 1:00 AM, activated the automatic door closer and passed out with the car still running. But the pitcher wasn't the only victim of the tragedy; his five-year-old son, Alex, who'd been sleeping upstairs, was also overcome by the toxic gas. Wilson's nine-year-old daughter, Denise, who'd also been sleeping in her upstairs bedroom, was found alive but in critical condition, and his wife, Bernice, had a broken jaw and was in shock.[3]

Wilson's death was officially ruled an accident and was never considered anything more than that. But what really happened in the early morning hours of Sunday, January 5, 1975 and how did the Wilson family arrive at that point?

Don Wilson grew up in Compton, California, a city that once spat out major league All-Stars at a regular rate, and attended Centennial High School, which produced several major leaguers, seven of whom were All-Stars.[4]

He moved on to Compton Junior College caught the eye of the Astros while playing semi-pro ball.[5] The Astros offered Wilson a $450-a-month contract but no bonus. "I've been told that the Yankees gave Phil Rizzuto a sandwich before signing him," he said. "I didn't even get a sandwich."[6] What the Astros got, though, was a very talented pitcher with a good head on his shoulders.

"Don has a great arm," said his first major league manager Grady Hatton in 1968. "He has a high-riding fast ball and a short, hard slider...He's young, strong and eager. He should be a dandy."[7] He also earned plaudits for his demeanor and intelligence. A.S. Doc Young of the *Los Angeles Sentinel* called Wilson, "Intelligent, articulate, concerned and competitive."[8]

The powerful righthander began his professional career in 1964 with the Colts of the Cocoa Rookie League, and blossomed in 1965 with the Cocoa Astros of the Class-A Florida State League, going 10–8 with a 1.44 ERA. He won 18 games for Amarillo in 1966, was named Pitcher of the Year and earned berths on the Texas League All-Star team and the AA All-West squad.

He was called up to the big leagues and made his major league debut on September 29, 1966 against the Cincinnati Reds, a team he would torment for the rest of his career. Wilson tossed six innings in relief and held on for his first major league win, a 3–2 victory.

He went only 10–9 in 1967, his rookie year, but with a 2.79 ERA and the aforementioned no-hitter. In mid-April, 1967 the pitcher earned votes from the United Press International's board of baseball experts as one of the top rookies heading into the campaign. He responded by breaking the Astros team record for consecutive scoreless innings when he logged his 25th on July 20 in a complete-game shutout over the Mets, prompting Mets skipper Wes Westrum to declare, "Don Wilson has the best arm I've seen all year."[9]

What made Wilson so difficult to hit was the movement on his fastball. "His fastball was fast, about 93, and it had fantastic movement—sometimes diving, sometimes sailing, sometimes breaking sharply out on a right-handed hitter," wrote Bill James in *The Neyer/James Guide to Pitchers*.

Wilson's pitching coach, Jim Owens, claimed that Wilson had the best high fastball in the league and that was how he recorded most of his strikeouts.[10] Wilson himself once told reporters that he could aim a fastball at a hitter's belt and by the time it reached the plate it would be at shoulder level.[11] Hyperbole, perhaps, but former big league hurler Dick Bosman told me much the same thing. "I was amazed at how hard he threw," Bosman explained in an e-mail. "It looked like the ball actually went up on the way to the plate! He threw so easy and the ball just exploded out of his hand."[12]

But Wilson felt he needed to improve his change-up or curveball to become a better pitcher. "If I can come up with the one other pitch, or even two, I think it would help me a lot because the hitter couldn't just lay back and wait for the fast ball and slider," Wilson said in November 1967.[13]

Working on a new pitch to add to his repertoire would be a recurring theme during Wilson's career, although James insists Wilson never mastered either. "Although he experimented with a curve and a changeup from 1967 until his death, neither of these pitches amounted to much," he wrote.[14]

Wilson's '68 season was marked by inconsistency and more health problems. He finished at 13–16 with a 3.28 ERA that was actually substandard in a league that averaged 2.99 for the entire year. Sometimes he was brilliant—he fanned 18 Reds on July 14 to become only the third pitcher in history to strike out that many in a nine-inning game, then whiffed 16 more Reds batters on September 10. Other times he was awful or just plain unlucky, like the time in early August when he tore a muscle in his rib cage after he sneezed too hard.[15]

In 1969 Wilson established career highs in wins (16), starts (34), innings (225) and strikeouts (235). But he also posted his worst ERA at 4.00, walked a then-career-high 97 batters and tossed a league-leading 16 wild pitches. He threw his second no-hitter on May 1, blanking the Cincinnati Reds only a day after Reds hurler Jim Maloney tossed a no-hitter at the Astros.

Wilson also made news off the field, mostly because of his friendship with first baseman Curt Blefary, which resulted in the two rooming together on road trips. Black and white teammates didn't room together until 1967 when Blefary and his black Baltimore teammate Sam Bowens roomed together on two road trips. It wasn't until 1969, though, that Wilson and Blefary became the first regularly integrated roommates in the majors.

"Blacks and whites have not been rooming together on the road in baseball," wrote Dick Young of the New York Daily News. "The long delay in integrated baseball rooming lists does not necessarily reflect a resistance by white players toward rooming with black players, although that is part of it. The other part is the resistance of black players toward rooming with white players."[16]

There was backlash from a few opposing players who couldn't believe Blefary would want to room with a "Negro," and the pair received funny looks in places like Atlanta and San Francisco.[17] But the biggest bombshell came in 1972 when Joe Morgan, who'd been traded to Cincinnati during the offseason, accused Astros manager Harry "The Hat" Walker of being "anti-black," claiming Walker didn't like him because of the color of his skin.[18]

"After he got over here [from Pittsburgh], he's only had trouble with the black players," Morgan told the Houston Post. "He had trouble with Dick Simpson from the start. He's had near fist fights and shouting matches with Don Wilson, Jim Wynn, me, Cesar Cedeno, Jay Alou and Marty Martinez." According to Morgan it was because of Walker's anti-black attitude that he was fired as Pirates manager after the players refused to play for him anymore.[19]

When Walker heard the allegations he responded, "If he feels this way, there must be some prejudice inside of him...My conscience is clear and I sleep good at night. I'm just sorry Joe feels that way. I don't."[20]

Walker being anti-black is debatable, however, especially when you consider that the skipper almost fielded the first all-black lineup in major league history when he sent eight black men onto the field in a game against Philadelphia in 1967, the lone exception being Denny Ribant, a white pitcher.

And he's received support from Hall of Fame hurler Bob Gibson, who credits Walker with encouraging him early in his career during Solly Hemus' reign as Cardinals manager.

Despite the career highs in wins and strikeouts, 1969 would prove to be Don Wilson's worst season in the big leagues. But Walker expected Wilson to give the Astros 15–20 more wins in 1970. Before the season got underway, however, Wilson suffered two setbacks. His buddy, Curt Blefary, was traded to the New York Yankees in December for flamboyant playboy Joe Pepitone, who'd worn out his welcome in New York.

Then Wilson's goal of getting through a season uninjured was shattered when tendonitis that cut his '69 season short landed him on the disabled list for most of the first three weeks of the '70 season. He didn't make his first start until May 2 and was ineffective at first, but he battled his way to a record of 11–6 with a 3.91 ERA. He was a different pitcher, though, fanning only 4.6 batters per nine innings, the lowest mark of his career.

According to Bill James, Wilson had to rely on his off-speed pitches to get by in 1970 and did "surprisingly well."[21] John Wilson corroborated that fact when he wrote about the pitcher "The big smoke was gone. Wilson was giving them soft stuff and curves.

Irv Young

Irv Young was known as "Young Cy" and "Cy The Second," but the only thing in common he had with legendary hurler Cy Young was his last name. Young did have an historic rookie season in 1905 with the Boston Beaneaters (Braves) when the 27-year-old southpaw paced the National League in innings (378), starts (42) and complete games (41). His innings and complete games totals are still a modern-day record for rookie pitchers.

On the other hand, he started his career by losing 20+ games in three straight seasons, and never finished any of his six seasons with a winning record, finishing his career at 63–95. Perhaps his most ignominious feat, however, was being on the only two teams to boast four 20-game losers, the Boston NL squad, who accomplished the feat in 1905 and 1906.

Many fans are aware that the 1920 Chicago White Sox and 1971 Baltimore Orioles had four 20-game winners, but few know about the futility of the '05-'06 Beaneaters. Vic Willis led the '05 team in losses with 29, followed by Kaiser Wilhelm, who went only 3–23, then by Chick Fraser (14–21), then by Young (20–21).

The following year Young was the only remaining member of the original 20-loss quartet, but the team managed to accomplish the feat again. Gus Dorner went 8–25, Young went 16–25, Vive Lindaman went 12–23 and Big Jeff Pfeffer went 13–22.

In 1907, the Boston NL club changed their name to "Doves," but that didn't help Young, who suffered his third straight 20-loss season, going 10–23. He tied a record also held by Casey Patten (1903–1905) and Fraser (1904–1906), who not only lost 20 games in three straight seasons, but managed to do it with three different teams.

No pitcher since Young has lost 20 games in three straight seasons.

There were only a few games he had enough of a fast ball to keep the hitters off balance."[22] Much to the delight of the Astros organization, however, Wilson regained his "old zip" prior to the '71 season and was healthy for the first time since 1969.

It was in 1971 that Wilson finally put it all together. He went 16–10 with a 2.45 ERA, increased his K/9 and paced the league in hits per nine innings. His record could have been even better, but he lost five games in which he threw at least seven innings and allowed two runs or less. Regardless, he was named to the National League All-Star team for the only time in his career.

The *Chicago Defender* was impressed. "If Houston's Don Wilson ever strikes the mother lode in his long search for consistency, he's bound to become one of baseball's golden pitchers," wrote the newspaper.[23] For his efforts Wilson was named the Astros' MVP by the Houston chapter of the Baseball Writers' Association of America. "I feel like we're going to win every time he goes out there," said Walker.[24]

The Astros hurler enjoyed another very good season in 1972, going 15–10 with a 2.68 ERA, but the consistency everyone raved about in 1971 was gone again, at least during the first half of the season. After starting the season at 5–7, Wilson went 10–3 in his last 13 decisions. He also recorded the team's 82nd victory on September 27 for new manager Leo Durocher, who'd replaced Harry Walker in late August after the Astros fell nine games out of first place.

In the offseason, Wilson blamed Houston's five-man rotation for his lack of consistency, but he expected to have his best year in 1973, mostly because the Astros were expected to go back to a four-man rotation. They did, but Wilson suffered through one of his worst seasons as a pro, going 11–16.

He posted a respectable 3.20 ERA, set a career high with 37 appearances and even recorded a pair of saves, the only two of his career, but it was a disappointing season, nonetheless. Wilson also had off-the-field issues. In late July, the pitcher was fined $300 and threatened with suspension when he called Durocher an "uncomplimentary" name as he boarded the team bus at Houston Intercontinental Airport. "Durocher was sitting at the front of the bus and Wilson reportedly made the remark as he passed Durocher on the way to his seat," reported the *Baltimore Sun*. "The Houston manager apparently was not sure he heard right, a sportswriter said, and asked the pitcher to repeat his comment. Wilson did so several times."[25]

A.S. Doc Young called 1973, Wilson's "summer of discontent" and speculated that he might be pitching elsewhere in 1974 after the name-calling incident with Durocher.[26] In fact, it was a summer of discontent for most of the Astros squad. Durocher started the '73 campaign off with a bang by pulling his players from a meeting with Players' Association executive director Marvin Miller in March, then fired pitching coach Jim Owens on the eve of the season. Only two weeks after the season got under way, Durocher was hospitalized with diverticulitis. He returned to the team, then announced in July that he was canceling batting practice for the remainder of the season because it wasn't the same as facing live pitching. After guiding the Astros to a record of 82–80, Durocher stepped down after only one season and was replaced by third base coach Preston Gomez.

But Wilson's run-ins with Walker and Durocher can't be laid entirely at the managers' feet. According to Astros third baseman Doug Rader, Wilson had become bitter and wasn't the same man with whom he played in the minors and early on in the majors.

"What made him bitter? I'd say he was a little disillusioned with people," explained Rader. "He was a very sensitive warm person, and very often the bad element in some people would disappoint him tremendously...A lotta [sic] people thought Don Wilson was a militant, but it wasn't true. He was just a very defensive

Don Wilson.

individual."[27] Teammate Bob Watson explained that Wilson was just misunderstood. "A lot of people didn't like Don Wilson because he spoke his mind. That was his way of letting people know he was a man. He had his opinions and he stuck to them."[28]

One person Wilson liked was Gomez, the team's new skipper. Gomez managed the San Diego Padres from 1969 to 1971 and the first 11 games of 1972, and gained some notoriety when he pinch hit for Clay Kirby on July 21, 1970 although Kirby was eight innings into a no-hitter.

Gomez joined the Astros coaching staff in 1973 and often managed the team in Durocher's absence. The new Houston pilot chose to go with a four-man rotation, even though the team had five solid starters in Wilson, Larry Dierker, Dave Roberts, Tom Griffin and veteran southpaw Claude Osteen, who'd come over from the Dodgers in a trade. Wilson ended up being the odd man out and began the season in the bullpen, making only one start in the team's first 30 games.

He didn't get his second start until May 12 but made the most of it, fanning 14 Cincinnati Reds in a 4–2 loss. That performance by itself launched him back into the rotation. "There's no way he can't be in there now," said Astros pitching coach Roger Craig. "Not the way he pitched against the Reds...That was the Wilson of old out there...If Don can sustain that type of pitching, he can beat anybody in the league."[29]

He began to whittle away at his ERA but over his next eight starts through June, he was maddeningly inconsistent. "An articulate 29-year-old, Wilson has fallen short of the greatness many predicted for him in his early days in the big time," wrote Larry Bortstein.[30]

His start on September 4, however, would prove to be arguably the most frustrating one of his career. The fourth-place Astros hosted the second-place Reds, who were only two-and-a-half games behind the division-leading Dodgers. Meanwhile Houston was 15 games out of first with only 27 left to play. Since many of Wilson's most memorable performances had come against the Reds, it was no surprise when he began dominating them again.

Through three innings, the only man to reach base against Wilson was George Foster who was hit by a pitch. Wilson walked former teammate Joe Morgan in the fourth, then surrendered two more walks in the fifth and allowed two unearned runs on an error by shortstop Roger Metzger. He walked Johnny Bench in the sixth, but escaped the inning on a pop out and a double play, then set the Reds down in order in the seventh. The Astros cut the lead to 2–1 in the bottom of the seventh, then Wilson sandwiched three more outs around another Morgan free pass.

With the pitcher due to lead off the bottom of the eighth, Gomez had a decision to make. Although Wilson had surrendered five walks and hit a batter, he had yet to allow a hit and was within three outs of his third career no-hitter. But the Astros were down to their last six outs and were still losing 2–1. Just as he'd done in 1970 with Clay Kirby, Gomez replaced Wilson with a pinch hitter. Ironically, Kirby was sitting in the opposing dugout watching the drama unfold, having been traded to the Reds during the offseason.

The Astrodome crowd of only 8,024 booed "lustily" when Tommy Helms was announced as Wilson's pinch-hitter. Helms grounded out to short, and a Houston rally was cut short on a strike-'em-out, throw-'em-out double play to end the inning. Relief pitcher Mike Cosgrove lost the no-hitter in the ninth and the Astros lost the game when Reds starter Jack Billingham set them down in order in the ninth.

"I get paid for winning the ball game not the no-hitter," Gomez explained after the game. "This was not one of my toughest decisions. The name of the game is to win." Reds manager Sparky Anderson defended Gomez. "If I had not done what Preston did, I wouldn't have been able to look baseball people in the face," said Anderson. "I would have had to retire if I let Wilson bat."[31] Some tried to make light of the situation; "Preston Gomez has broken up more no-hitters than Ty Cobb," quipped Jim Murray of the *L.A. Times*."[32]

Newspapers reported that Wilson was "apparently upset over his removal," and couldn't be reached for comment. Milton Richman wrote that Wilson was hanging out in the trainer's room, having a beer and avoiding the media, with whom he didn't want to speak.[33] Not only was he attempting to become only the second National League hurler with three no-hitters, joining Sandy Koufax on that very short list, but he was about to become the first pitcher in baseball history to toss two no-hitters against the same opponent, in this case the Cincinnati Reds. After cooling off, Wilson defended his manager's decision. "I respect Preston Gomez more than ever tonight," Wilson told reporters. "When people start putting personal goals ahead of the team, you'll never have a winner. I understand how Preston feels. He is consistent and I have nothing but admiration for him."[34]

But Richman reported that Wilson's wife, Bernice, was angry that her husband had been pulled from the game.[35] And Bill Nunn Jr. of the *Pittsburgh Courier* claimed that friends of Wilson described the pitcher as being "furious" that he wasn't given the opportunity to complete the no-hitter.[36]

Wilson fell to 10–11 with the loss and finished the season at 11–13 with a 3.08 ERA. His last appearance of the '74 campaign was a complete-game two-hit shutout over the Braves, and would prove to be the final one of his career. Ironically, the pitcher who once fanned a record-tying 18 batters in one game, recorded no strikeouts in his final performance.

On January 6, 1975 newspapers carried the tragic news of Wilson's death. The 29-year-old pitcher and his five-year-old son, Alex, had succumbed to asphyxia due to carbon monoxide after Wilson passed out with his 1972 Thunderbird's motor running in the sealed attached garage located directly beneath the bedrooms where his family slept. According to reports, Bernice called a neighbor in the early afternoon hours of January 5 and said she needed help. Apparently she had been awakened by the running motor and went to check on her kids, who "sounded like they were crying in their sleep." Bernice picked up Alex and carried him into the master bedroom, then shut the doors of both the master bedroom and her nine-year-old daughter, Denise's, room.

She tried to go back to sleep but the running motor kept her awake, so she went to the garage to investigate and found Don. When she failed to find a pulse on her husband, Bernice called the fire department. She and her daughter were rushed to Southwest Memorial Hospital where Bernice was found to be in shock with a fractured left jaw, but in fair condition. Denise was in a coma and was transferred to Texas Children's Hospital in critical condition.

When police arrived at the Wilson residence, they found Don in the passenger seat of his car. "His head was tilted back resting on the seat, and his arms were at his sides," reported the *New York Times*. "His left foot was crossed over his right foot. A pack of cigarettes was on the dashboard in front of Wilson. The left front door was closed, but the right front door was open. The ignition was on and the gasoline indicator was at empty, but the car's engine was cold."[37]

"Details of the deaths are still sketchy but the preliminary investigation indicates the deaths are accidental," said a police homicide spokesman. "That is all we know now. An autopsy has been ordered. Perhaps more on the death and Mrs. Wilson's injury can be released tomorrow."[38]

Although Wilson's death resembled a suicide and has been reported as such by various sources, no one who knew Wilson actually believed he killed himself. "Don had everything going for him. He had it all together," said fellow Houston hurler Dave Roberts. "We had been working at the speaker's bureau together and everything was fine."[39] The Astros speaker's bureau arranged speaking engagements for the players and employed Wilson and Roberts during the offseason. The last time Roberts saw Wilson was at the bureau's office on December 15. But others, like Astros publicity director, Bobby Risinger, claimed they had seen Wilson at the offices several times over the winter and that he was looking forward to the 1975 season.

"He really was enthused about the upcoming season," Risinger said. "We were looking over some of his statistics from last year and he said he thought he could win 20 games this season. That meant a lot to Don, to win 20 games."[40]

"The most heartbreaking thing to me, the shame of it all," said Doug Rader, "is that he had overcome his bitterness, and he was now again the man he used to be, the one I knew at first...I've heard all kinds of crazy things, rumors, about how Don Wilson died. I don't care what anyone says, I'll never believe he killed himself. He loved life too much. His death simply had to be an accident. I'd stake my life on that."[41]

The day after Wilson was found dead in his car, Harris County medical examiner, Dr. Joseph Jachimcyzk, found an excess of 60% of carbon monoxide in Wilson's blood. The autopsy also found that the pitcher's blood/alcohol level was .167, well above the .10 legal limit in Texas.

His daughter was still in a coma and it was reported that Bernice, didn't have a fractured jaw, it was merely bruised, swollen and painful. Detective Jim Pierce opined that the deaths were accidental. "I don't see how it could have been anything else," he said. "There were no signs of violence at all."[42]

So what about Bernice's jaw? She first told the attending physician that she had no idea how she suffered her injury. Then she said she thought she might have been struck. Finally, she claimed that she had fallen against a wall a few days prior to her husband's death. Her story about that evening's events also changed slightly, or at least the reports changed, but she was heavily sedated at the time and was "unable to give officers a complete account of the incident." The *New York Times* reported that Bernice had been awakened by her children crying in their sleep and it was then that she heard the running car engine. She "wiped the childrens' faces with a cool cloth and returned to bed," the *Times* wrote, mentioning nothing about her picking up Alex and carrying him to the master bedroom. When she couldn't get back to sleep, Bernice went to the garage and found Don in his car with all the doors locked.[43]

On January 7 the *Hartford Courant* reported more details about the case. Dr. Sheldon Green, Harris County assistant medical examiner, said Wilson had been dead several hours before he was found, which makes sense considering police speculated he arrived home around 1:00 AM and wasn't discovered by Bernice until more than 12 hours later. "Exhaust stains found on the garage floor indicated the car had been running for some time," wrote the *Courant*. "It was out of gas and the battery was dead." As for Bernice's injured jaw, Detective Doc Fults stated, "That's being investigated now. We don't have any other information yet. Detectives are at the house now."[44]

A day later homicide detectives said they were unable to rule Wilson's death accidental because of "unanswered questions." One of those questions involved Bernice's jaw, which according to her physician was not broken, fractured or bruised; it was swollen from an "infected salivary gland at the jaw and ear," the fourth explanation about the status of her bruised face.[45] Meanwhile, Denise was still in critical condition.

Memorial services were held for Don and Alex on January 9 in Houston, then the funeral was held in Faithful Central Baptist Church in Los Angeles the next day. Father and son were buried in Forest Lawn Memorial Park in Covina Hills, California.

On January 16 the *Corpus Christi Times* reported that Bernice was no longer cooperating with homicide officers and was referring all questions to her attorney, Richard "Racehorse" Haynes. Homicide detective, Larry Ott, said "so far as the police are concerned the case was an accident but authorities wish to clear up various elements in the story."[46] Howie Evans of the *New York Amsterdam News* wondered whether Bernice's "infected" jaw was actually caused by a domestic dispute just prior to Wilson's death. "It was a known fact that Wilson and his spouse weren't exactly hitting it off," Evans wrote on January 18. "Could it be Wilson and his spouse argued in the car, he popped her, and in his less than sober state remained in the car with the motor running? We'll never know."[47]

Finally, on February 5, 1975 Dr. Jachimcyzk officially ruled that the deaths of Don and Alex Wilson were accidental. Detective Ott concurred. "I have found no evidence during the investigation that would indicate murder and certainly no evidence that would indicate suicide." Bernice was of little help to investigators and began "claiming amnesia for that Saturday and Sunday evening Jan. 4 and also for events early Sunday leading up to the time that the bodies were found."[48]

Denise finally awoke from her coma and recovered, but even though her father's death was ruled accidental, not everyone was buying it. "Wilson's death is still steeped in controversy," wrote the *Chicago Defender*. "But there are some who still have their doubts."[49]

Wilson's number 40 was retired by the Houston Astros and the team wore black patches on their left sleeve in tribute to their fallen teammate.

"Don Wilson never won more than 16 games in a season," wrote Bill Christine of the *Pittsburgh Post Gazette*. "His lifetime record in the big leagues was 103–92 [*sic*]. That's not enough to get a pitcher into the Hall of Fame. But off the field he was something special."[50]

Ray Fisher's Revenge

Ray Fisher.

In 1921 Reds pitcher Ray Fisher was banned for life for contract jumping after he signed a deal to play for the Reds, accepted more money to coach at the University of Michigan,[1] then entertained an offer from an outlaw league that had several blacklisted players on its rosters.

He admitted talking to the outlaw team and when Reds manager Pat Moran refuted Fisher's claim that he had given the pitcher permission to visit the Michigan campus and mull over the university's job offer, Commissioner Kenesaw Mountain Landis banned him for life. It was a decision David Pietrusza called "perhaps his least popular," and one which historian Harold Seymour called "incomprehensible."

Fisher served as Michigan's head coach for 38 years and led the team to a championship in 1953. He was reinstated to good standing in 1980 by Commissioner Bowie Kuhn, and honored at Yankee Stadium in 1982 as the oldest living Yankee.

The Promising Life and Tragic Death of Austin McHenry

By the time he was 25 years old, St. Louis Cardinals outfielder Austin McHenry was considered one of baseball's best outfielders and hitters, especially after enjoying a 1921 season that saw him finish with a .350 batting average, second only to teammate and future Hall of Famer Rogers Hornsby. McHenry also finished second to Hornsby in slugging at .531, placed among the top five National League hitters in doubles, home runs, RBIs, total bases, and extra-base hits, and was one of only six NL hitters with 200 hits that season. Blessed with a strong arm and an easy gait that was sometimes mistaken for indifference, McHenry was considered not only one of baseball's best outfielders and hitters after his remarkable 1921 campaign, but one of the ten best left fielders of all time to that point in baseball history. His performance tailed off in 1922 as he battled inconsistency at the plate and in the field, caused mostly by problems with his vision that had McHenry fearing he was going blind. Concerned about his health, Cardinals manager Branch Rickey sent McHenry to his Ohio home to rest, where it was discovered the star outfielder had a brain tumor. Tragically, he would lose his life only four months later.

Austin Bush McHenry was born on September 22, 1895 in Wrightsville, Ohio. He grew up in Jefferson Township and played baseball through high school, but it wasn't until 1914 when he came under the tutelage of scout Billy Doyle, who ran a baseball school for young players in Ohio, that he really began to show off his abilities. McHenry played the outfield where he found immediate success. "There he shone with brilliancy," wrote the *Portsmouth Daily Times*. "It seemed that no one could hit it over his head and he was a genius on coming in for short line-drives over the infield."[1]

Austin McHenry (R) with teammate and fellow slugger
Rogers Hornsby.

He signed his first professional contract with Portsmouth of the Class D Ohio State League in 1915 at the age of 19 and helped lead the Cobblers to a pennant. McHenry was gifted but raw. But what he lacked in knowledge he made up for with hustle, eagerness, enthusiasm, and a determination to succeed. Soon he was drawing comparisons to Ed Delahanty and Ty Cobb and was said to have "an arm of steel."[2] And he could flat out hit, prompting the *Portsmouth Daily Times* to call him a "veritable demon at the bat."[3]

McHenry's first season as a pro was a successful one as he batted .297 and slugged .421, and finished second on the team in home runs with four. He began the 1916 season with Portsmouth but was sold to the American Association's Milwaukee Brewers in July for $300. McHenry spent the rest of the season with the Brewers but struggled, hitting only .240 and slugging .326 in 72 games. He was also the victim of a beaning that seemed fairly innocuous at the time, especially since he was able to continue playing after a short rest, but would later be blamed for the tumor that eventually took his life.[4] McHenry was farmed out to Peoria of the Central League in the spring of 1917 and batted .270 with two homers before being recalled to Milwaukee where he batted .235 with four homers.

At first glance it looked like McHenry had another poor season, but only two of his teammates had as many home runs, and they had the benefit of 500-at-bat seasons, whereas McHenry recorded only 373 at-bats for the Brewers. In terms of at-bats per home run only Johnny Beall had a better season than McHenry, who was becoming one of the better home run hitters in the high minors. The Cincinnati Reds were clearly impressed and purchased McHenry's contract after the 1917 season for $2,500. But after he suffered a broken nose during a spring training game in 1918, he was returned to Milwaukee.

McHenry made the most of his situation and began depositing balls into the seats at a league-leading rate. He belted five homers in 170 at-bats to lead the American Association in home runs through June, which prompted the St. Louis Cardinals to acquire his services on June 12.[5] McHenry reported to the Cards and made his major league debut on June 22 in the first game of a doubleheader against the very team that released him earlier in the year. He failed to record a hit in two official at-bats (although he reached base when he was hit by a pitch from Reds hurler Pete Schneider), but he showed off his powerful arm and recorded two assists from left field. He also played in the second game and went 1-for-5, rapping out his first major league hit, a double, and scoring his first run.

He spent the rest of the 1918 season anchoring left field for the last-place Cardinals and proved to be a promising major leaguer.

He batted .261 with a homer and 29 RBIs in 272 at-bats and finished fourth on the team with six triples. And among the regulars only Bob Fisher (136) and Walton Cruise (134) posted a better OPS+ than McHenry's 109.[6] On defense he was a little shaky, but he made up for it with strong, accurate throws that resulted in 14 assists, placing him among the top 10 outfielders in the National League despite playing in only 80 games.

Although McHenry played well in 1918, he entered the 1919 campaign with little fanfare. Cardinals manager Branch Rickey had high hopes for McHenry, however, and ordered his coaches to spend additional time with the youngster hitting him fly balls and throwing him extra batting practice.[7] McHenry began the 1919 season as the team's fourth outfielder, occasionally spelling starters Cliff Heathcote, Burt Shotton, and Jack Smith, but mostly serving as a pinch-hitter and runner. He began to find more time in the starting lineup in late May and eventually unseated the injured Shotton as the starting left fielder.

The extra preseason work paid off. McHenry vastly improved his glove work and committed only three errors, finishing fourth among NL outfielders in fielding percentage, and recorded 20 assists, good for fifth in the league. He also improved at the plate, batting .286 and slugging .404, second on the Cards to Rogers Hornsby, and led the team with 11 triples, which placed him among the top 10 in the loop.

Others began to take notice. The Reds, realizing their earlier mistake, offered Rickey $25,000 for McHenry in September, but Rickey rejected the offer and insisted his prized outfielder would play for no one but the Cardinals.[8] A newspaper report in early September gushed about McHenry's play, calling him "one of the most talented outfielders to break into fast company in some years." Sportswriter Frank Menke observed that all of the phenoms that joined the NL around the same time as McHenry were back in

Smead Jolley

Smead "Smudge" Jolley was one of the greatest minor league hitters of all time, and also had a successful major league career, albeit a short one. Jolley finished his 16-year minor league career with 3,043 hits, 336 home runs and a .367 batting average.

His best season was arguably the 1928 campaign when he batted .404 with 309 hits, 52 doubles and 45 homers in 191 games for the Pacific Coast League's San Francisco Seals.

Prior to the 1930 season, White Sox owner Charles Comiskey purchased Jolley for $50,000 and he rewarded the "Old Roman" by hitting .313 with 16 homers and 114 RBIs in his rookie season at age 28. Unfortunately he couldn't field and became infamous for making three errors on one play, although that's never been corroborated.

He was traded to the Boston Red Sox in 1932 and had his best season, batting .312 with 18 homers and 106 RBIs (118 OPS+), which placed him 24th in MVP voting, but he was terrible in the field again. He spent one more year in Boston before being traded to the St. Louis Browns in December 1933. The same day, he was dealt to the Hollywood Stars of the PCL, and he spent the rest of his career in the minors.

Had he been able to field or run, Jolley might have been one of the best MLB hitters of his generation, but he had to be content with being one of the best in minor league history.

the minors while the Cardinals outfielder was one of the "reigning sensations" of the big leagues.

McHenry earned a starting nod in 1920 and split his time between left and center field in a makeshift St. Louis outfield that had five players shuttling in and out of the lineup, including Heathcote who had yet to live up to his hype. But McHenry's stint in St. Louis almost became short lived when he contemplated a jump to the Agathon Steel team, a Massilon, Ohio semi-pro industrial league team led by former Federal League catcher George Textor.[9] At the time, industrial league teams were luring current and former major and minor leaguers and those with major league aspirations by offering them jobs and major league level salaries. Textor followed the Cardinals to Boston and offered McHenry a contract, but Rickey learned about the negotiations and put a stop to them before he could lose his prized outfielder.

Despite a decrease in OPS+ and fielding percentage in 1920, McHenry enjoyed another productive season, establishing career highs in several categories. He batted .282 with a team-leading 10 home runs and 65 RBIs, and slugged a career-best .423. He also recorded 21 assists, good for sixth in the league. Only Cy Williams, Irish Meusel, and George "Highpockets" Kelly hit more home runs than McHenry in the National League. After belting only two round-trippers in his first 643 major league at-bats, McHenry was suddenly among the top sluggers in baseball.

It helped that a new era in baseball had just begun. The Deadball Era had come to an end in 1920, partly due to the ban on the spitball, and home runs were up 26% across the league and 41% across the majors. The days of "small ball," in which teams manufactured runs with bunts, steals, and the hit-and-run were giving way to more potent methods of scoring ushered in by Babe Ruth in the American League and Williams, Kelly, Hornsby and McHenry in the National.

By May 1921, the *New York Times* railed about a home run "epidemic" sweeping through the majors and warned that records would tumble by season's end, blaming the onslaught on a new "livelier" ball: "It is true that the restrictions which were imposed upon pitchers, starting with the opening of the 1920 pennant races and still in force, have made hitting easier, but even this does not explain the great advance in home run hitting. The fact that many players who seldom hit for the circuit have branched out as long distance sluggers is not explained satisfactorily by changes in pitching rules. They are no stronger physically than before, yet their drives are carrying far beyond the former limits."[10]

In St. Louis the boost in four-baggers was especially obvious in the batting lines of first baseman Jack Fournier, who had five as of May 23, after hitting only three the year before and posting a career-high six in 1914, and McHenry, who had four circuit clouts in only 93 at-bats, putting him on pace to hit 25 over a full season.

McHenry didn't hit 25 home runs in 1921, but he finished the season with a career-high 17 to go along with a .350 batting average and 102 runs batted in. He also recorded his first 200-hit season, and set career highs in runs, doubles, steals, walks, on-base percentage, and slugging. It proved to be a special year for the 25-year-old up-and-coming star as he finished second in the batting race to his teammate Hornsby, second in slugging, also to Hornsby, third in RBIs, fourth in home runs, and fifth in doubles. And the team was getting better as well, finishing at 87–66 and in third place, after finishing no higher than fifth over the three previous seasons.

McHenry's 1921 campaign was so impressive that he was named one of the 10 best left fielders of all-time by an anonymous source cryptically referred to by The Sporting News as "one of the most highly regarded of Eastern baseball critics."[11]

"This is interesting, as it shows a growing appreciation of the real worth of this sterling player. He has not in the past received all that is his due. Even in St. Louis the fans...probably have not rated him as he deserves. His work is not of the spectacular sort, he does not furnish great thrills. If he goes far afield for a long drive he ambles over the ground with a stride that makes it appear he is just out for practice. McHenry is without a question one of the game's greatest outfielders. And he is one of the game's greatest hitters."[12]

Giants manager John McGraw was so impressed with his 1921 showing that he reportedly offered Rickey $50,000 for McHenry over the winter, but the Cards' exec refused to budge.[13] Hornsby and McHenry were two of the league's best hitters, and "Spittin' Bill" Doak anchored an improving pitching staff that also featured future Hall of Famer Jesse Haines and 25-year-old Bill Sherdel. If the Cardinals were to topple the Giants in the upcoming pennant race, they'd need all of their best players to do it.

But tragedy struck the team in late January 1922 when catcher Pickles Dillhoefer contracted typhoid fever. He remained in the hospital for a little more than three weeks but never recovered, dying on February 23 at the age of 28.

Spring training had barely just begun when news of Dillhoefer's death reached camp. It was the second time in four years that McHenry had lost a friend and former Portsmouth teammate. Once he settled back into playing ball, though, McHenry got off to a nice start with a home run on March 7 and was looking to repeat his 1921 performance. When the regular season started he picked up right where he left off the season before, recording hits in each of his first six games and batting .348 through April 18. He also recorded two assists in his first two games. By the end of April he was hitting .310 and slugging .483 and had seven extra-base hits in 15 games. He wasn't quite as good in May, though, and after hitting four homers in his first 26 games in 1921, McHenry had only two after 43 games in 1922.

But as the weather heated up in June, so did McHenry's bat. In the month's first nine games, McHenry batted .485 with 10 runs, six doubles, and two homers, and he enjoyed a stretch from June 6 to June 12, in which he recorded at least two hits in each game and batted .542. By mid-June, the Cards' budding superstar had his average up to .332 and was slugging at a .511 clip. For all intents and purposes, it looked like McHenry was on his way to duplicating his breakout 1921 season. But he couldn't sustain his torrid pace and batted only .191 in his last 11 June contests. At the end of the month, he was batting .306 with five homers, slugging .474, and was on pace to post numbers that would have fallen neatly in between his last two seasons, not as good as 1921 but better than 1920. Regardless, most of the Cards' faithful were unimpressed and began to boo McHenry. Only the kids refrained from razzing the outfielder. "When he got back near the knothole gang, they cheered him as they always had," recalled Rickey. "Men abandon their friends in the give and take of ordinary industry, but boys are always loyal to their heroes."[14]

Finally something happened in late June that concerned Rickey and proved to be more serious than anyone fathomed. In a game against the Reds on June 26, Rickey noticed McHenry was struggling to catch fly balls and asked his outfielder if he was okay. "Yes, I feel alright," McHenry assured his manager, "but I can't see. I don't know what it is. Maybe I'm going blind."[15] Rickey removed McHenry from the game, then ordered McHenry back to his home in Blue Creek, Ohio to rest. According to McHenry's friend and former mentor, Billy Doyle, the spot above McHenry's left temple where he'd been hit by a pitch in 1916 had become sore again six years later and had affected McHenry's eyesight. Doyle would later insist it was the beaning that caused the tumor that resulted in McHenry's death.[16]

McHenry stayed in Blue Creek until late July when he rejoined the Cardinals in New York for a series against the Giants. He made his last start on July 28 in the first game of a doubleheader, going 0-for-4 and recording a putout in the field. Three days later, on July 31, he made his last major league appearance, pinch hitting for Jack Smith in the seventh inning of St. Louis' 6–2 victory over Brooklyn. McHenry singled in his final big league at-bat and drove in a run, then left the game for a pinch runner. Despite his successful turn at the plate, Rickey could see that McHenry was still ill and sent him home again.

On August 10, Hugh Fullerton reported that McHenry wouldn't be back with St. Louis in 1922.[17] At the time, the Cardinals stood in first place and sported a slim one and a half game lead over the second-place Giants. But it took only two days for the Giants to claim the lead in the National League, and by the end of August, the Cards found themselves six and a half games off the pace and battling the Chicago Cubs for second place, leaving Rickey lamenting the loss of McHenry.

"[The Cardinals] are a club that needs a lot of runs to win," Rickey told reporters. "It didn't get them on the last eastern trip. [Rogers] Hornsby fell off a bit in hitting. [Jack] Fournier's fielding became so unsteady that I had to get him out of there and McHenry was so ill that I sent him home. Of the three McHenry's absence I think was the most disastrous."[18]

McHenry was finally admitted to Good Samaritan Hospital in Cincinnati where doctors discovered that the fallen player had a brain tumor and would need a risky operation to remove it. The news was devastating but the God-fearing McHenry seemed resigned to his fate, telling relatives, "It seems hard that so young a man as I must die, but I am ready when the Master summons me." Prior to surgery, he told Rickey, who had become a good friend, that he felt like he was up to bat with the bases loaded and a 3–2 count, but promised to "hit at the next one."[19]

McHenry went under the knife on October 19, but the whole tumor couldn't be removed due to its location. Regardless, it was hoped McHenry would make a full recovery. Less than a month after the operation, however, McHenry was sent home from the hospital on November 22 with no hope of recovery.

Five days later, McHenry died at his home in Blue Creek on November 27 with his wife Ethel, daughter Leone, and son Bush at his side. Upon hearing the news of McHenry's death, Rickey issued a statement to the press: "We do not look upon the death of Austin as that of a ballplayer, but as a dear friend. He was one of our most popular players, and was a particular favorite of the younger fans, especially the young boys."[20]

The Sporting News was equally eloquent. "No ball club ever had a more loyal player and there are few outfielders in the game today who are as good as McHenry was at his best. His death is a distinct loss to baseball."

McHenry was laid to rest in Moore's Chapel Cemetery next to a church that overlooked his home. He was only 27 years old.

Remembering Denny Galehouse

With three games left in the 1948 season the Cleveland Indians held a two game lead over both the Boston Red Sox and New York Yankees, but losses to the Detroit Tigers in two of their final three contests and a two-game sweep by the Red Sox over the Yankees gave Cleveland and Boston identical 96–58 records to close out the season on October 3. Boston was buzzing about a potential World Series match-up between the Red Sox and the National League's Braves, but the Sox had to defeat the Indians one last time to advance to the Series.

Prior to the playoff game newspapers were speculating about which pitchers would be tabbed to face off in the crucial game. Some suspected 19-game winner Bob Feller would get the call for Cleveland despite having pitched the previous day against the Tigers. Feller lasted only 2 1/3 innings against Detroit in a 7–1 loss and he apparently had something left in his tank. Most figured 20-game winner Bob Lemon would get the ball. Lemon last pitched on October 1 in a 5–3 loss to Detroit and he would have been better rested than Feller, although not much. Lemon paced the junior circuit in innings pitched and complete games, so he had the arm to withstand the workload, and he had almost twice as many shutouts (10) as the runner up. Either way, Indians manager and shortstop Lou Boudreau was playing it close to the vest.

Meanwhile Boston manager Joe McCarthy had a decision of his own to make. Mel Parnell, a 26-year-old southpaw who fashioned a 15–8 record and posted a team-leading 3.14 ERA in his first full season, seemed to be the obvious choice. He'd last pitched on September 30, beating the Senators 7–3, and would have been working on three days' rest. Jack Kramer, who paced the team with 18 wins, and Joe Dobson, who won 16 games on the year, had pitched

Boston to wins over the Yankees during the previous two days, so neither would have been at full strength. That left Ellis Kinder, a 10-game winner who was fully rested, Mickey Harris, who went 7–10 with a 5.30 ERA in 17 starts, and Denny Galehouse, a 36-year-old journeyman hurler who'd gone 8–8 with a 4.00 earned run average in 1948, and had more losses than wins in his 15-year career.

When asked who he intended to start, McCarthy admitted he had no idea. "I had everybody working in the bullpen this afternoon and I haven't the ghost of an idea who I'll start tomorrow. I'll try to dream up a starter tonight."[1] Indeed McCarthy had ordered several of his hurlers to continue warming up in the bullpen, including Galehouse, in Boston's 10–5 win over the Yankees on the season's final day. He was afraid Joe DiMaggio and company might stage a late rally and wanted to make sure he had warm arms to come into the game if needed. Unfortunately the extra work taxed Boston's staff. It appeared that no one would be ready to throw for the Red Sox the following day.

Boudreau surprised everyone when he named 27-year-old Gene Bearden as his starter. It wasn't that Bearden didn't earn the assignment. On the contrary, Bearden had won 19 games to that point and would win his first ERA title with a microscopic 2.42 ERA, which was almost a half-run better than everyone else. But the left-handed knuckleballer had thrown only two days before in an 8–0 whitewash of the Tigers and had only one day to rest. Still Boudreau had faith in the rookie and well he should. Bearden had won his previous six starts, allowing no more than three runs in any of them, and was coming off consecutive shutouts. Despite making his decision well before game time, Boudreau kept it from the Red Sox until 13 minutes before game time when Bearden started warming up.

McCarthy could have and probably should have countered with his own left-handed ace, Parnell, but he feared the combination of

Fenway Park's short left field porch and Cleveland's right-hand heavy lineup would mitigate Parnell's effectiveness. Instead McCarthy shocked everyone when he tabbed Galehouse to get the start.

The *Sporting News* didn't quibble with McCarthy's choice. "Denny [Galehouse] is known as a money pitcher," wrote the paper. "He was well rested and once earlier in the summer he had held the Indians to two hits in eight and two thirds innings." Galehouse had pitched in the postseason for the St. Louis Browns in 1944 and was very good, splitting his two decisions, and posting a 1.50 ERA in two complete game performances.

Denny Galehouse.

What *TSN* failed to mention, however, was that Galehouse had also been pasted by the Indians on August 25—he allowed nine runs in only five innings—and he'd lasted only four innings in his last start, which came on September 18. On paper, Galehouse was certainly the most rested of Boston's starters, but he admitted years later that he'd thrown the equivalent of six innings while warming up in the bullpen the day before on Joe McCarthy's orders. It's doubtful the Red Sox skipper realized he'd had Galehouse warming up so long, but Galehouse followed orders and continued warming up from the fourth inning on. Now he was getting a start in the most crucial game of the season.

Nobody had any inkling that Galehouse would be taking the ball against Cleveland. Parnell went to bed early the night before, assuming he'd be getting the start. Kinder was the only member of the regular rotation who was fully rested. Yet neither was tabbed by McCarthy to pitch the most important game of the year.

"We just couldn't understand it," catcher Matt Batts explained. "It wasn't logical at the time. We had Parnell ready to go, and Kinder was ready. I would say 100% of the players were against [Galehouse starting]." Still the Red Sox were favored to win and the players were confident. When outfielder Wally Moses guessed aloud that Lemon would most likely get the start for Cleveland, Ted Williams bellowed, "I don't care if he's beaten us twenty games this year. We'll knock his brains out tomorrow."

The teams were evenly matched. Boston led the league in runs, doubles, walks, and on base percentage. Cleveland was first in home runs and batting average. The Indians had the better pitching staff, pacing the loop in ERA with a 3.22 mark that was more than a run better than Boston's, but the Red Sox had a decent staff, finishing second in complete games, third in runs allowed per game, and fourth in ERA. And the two teams finished first and second, respectively, in fielding with Cleveland taking top honors. The Red Sox boasted a powerful lineup that featured Williams in left (.369/25/127), Vern Stephens at shortstop (.269/29/137), and Bobby Doerr at second base (.285/27/111), but the Indians were even more impressive. Six Cleveland batters finished the year with at least 14 home runs and Joe Gordon and Ken Keltner belted more than 30 each. Boudreau batted .355, left fielder Dale Mitchell hit .336, and center fielder Larry Doby hit .301.

The game got underway at 1:30 and McCarthy's decision to start Galehouse proved to be terrible from the outset. Mitchell led off the game and slammed a high drive that Williams caught in front of the Green Monster for the first out. Allie Clark, who'd batted .310 with nine homers in 271 at-bats during the season and earned his only start of the season at first base, grounded out to Johnny

Pesky at short to give Galehouse and the Sox two quick outs. But Boudreau stepped into a Galehouse offering and deposited it into the screen above the Green Monster in left-center field to give the Indians a quick 1-0 lead. Gordon grounded out to end the inning.

Boston responded in earnest, however, and plated a run of their own in the bottom of the frame. After Dom DiMaggio grounded out, Pesky poled a double to right-center. Williams grounded out, but Stephens laced a two-out single down the left field line to score Pesky to knot the score at one apiece.

Early on, the veteran Galehouse was actually outpitching his rookie counterpart. Except for the Boudreau homer, a Keltner single in the second and a walk to Bearden in the third, the Red Sox hurler had cruised through the Indians lineup and hadn't allowed a Cleveland batter past first base. He needed a little help from his defense, though, which DiMaggio provided with a shoestring catch of what should have been a single for Doby (Arthur Daly wrote of the play, "Only two center fielders in the game could have made that catch. Both of them are named DiMaggio"). Meanwhile Bearden issued two walks and a single in the second inning, but the Red Sox failed to score.

Both men pitched well in the third, but Galehouse finally tired in the fourth and the Indians took control of the game. Boudreau and Gordon singled to lead off the fourth and McCarthy ordered Kinder to begin warming up. Alas, it was too late as Keltner smashed a three-run homer to left to give the Indians a 4-1 lead. That was it for Galehouse. Kinder came on in relief and immediately surrendered a double to Doby, who eventually scored Cleveland's fifth run after a sacrifice bunt and a ground out.

The Red Sox had no answer in the fourth and Boudreau homered again in the fifth to give Cleveland a 6-1 edge. Boston cut Cleveland's lead in half when Doerr ripped a two-run homer in the bottom of the sixth, but that was all the offense the Red Sox could muster as Bearden settled down and allowed only one more hit, a Williams single in the eighth, the rest of the way. The Indians tacked on solo runs in the eighth and ninth to make the final score 8–3 and send Cleveland to its first World Series since 1920.

The *New York Times*' Arthur Daley summed up the game in poetic fashion:

"High-powered master-minding, strategic concepts, and Machiavellian managerial maneuvering are awesomely impressive—when they work. Marse Joe McCarthy carefully studied the wind which blew out toward the short left field fence today and abandoned all notion of using his stylish young southpaw, Mel Parnell. Instead, he gambled on the ancient Denny Galehouse, a cutie on the hill who uses guile in place of speed.

However, Lou Boudreau, who probably doesn't know any better, risked everything on his stylish young southpaw, Gene Bearden. Fenway Park is supposed to be poison on left-handed pitchers, particularly when the wind blows the wrong way. But Bearden fed the poison in large doses to the Red Sox and killed their pennant chances."

Cleveland went on to face the Boston Braves in the World Series and broke the city's heart completely when they defeated the Braves in six games. Meanwhile McCarthy escaped indictment--Red Sox owner Tom Yawkey declared, "I'd rather finish second with Joe McCarthy than first with someone else" and all of the blame for Boston's loss fell squarely on Galehouse's shoulders. Red Sox fans howled and demanded he be traded. Galehouse stayed with the team and appeared in only two games the following season, throwing two innings, and posting an ugly 13.50 ERA. He was released on May 11, 1949 and never pitched in another major league game.

Chalmer "Bill" Cissell:
The $123,000 Lemon

Chalmer Cissell came from a long line of Missouri ballplayers and followed in their footsteps, playing third base for the Perryville team when he was 14, then high school and semi-pro ball before quitting school and enlisting with the Second Cavalry at Fort Riley, Kansas in 1922.

It was while playing baseball for the army in 1925 that he was discovered by Des Moines of the Class A Western League, who bought Cissell's release and signed him to a contract.

Demons manager Shano Collins insisted that Cissell was one of the greatest, if not the greatest young player he had ever seen. Cissell batted .345 before being sold to Portland of the Pacific Coast League for a reported $13,000 and two unnamed players. It was alleged to have been the highest price ever paid by one minor league team to another.

He broke out in 1927 and became one of the best hitting short-stops in the PCL. On defense he committed 76 errors, but sports-writer John B. Foster chalked that up to effort. "His error column was big, but a wise manager will take a player who tries in prefer-ence to one who ambles after none but the easy ones." In fact, his hustle, impressive range, and wiry 160-pound frame earned him the nickname "Spider."

In early November the Chicago White Sox acquired Cissell for what was valued at $123,000. Portland received $75,000 in cash and two players—outfielder Ike Boone and southpaw Bert Cole. The deal was a record at the time, surpassing the $100,000 the White Sox sent the San Francisco Seals for third baseman Willie Kamm in 1922. It wasn't long before Foster dubbed Cissell, the "$100,000 Beauty."

The pressure on Cissell was enormous, and he also faced off-the-field pressures and burdens; only two days after the deal was finalized, he found himself on the wrong side of a woman scorned, 20-year-old Bernice Ryner, who filed charges of seduction against Cissell. He was indicted and arrested on November 9.

According to Ryner, Cissell promised to marry her and she began making preparations to join him in Portland, but he failed to send her train fare. Then he promised to come to Des Moines but failed to appear. The bride-to-be was understandably upset; not only were Cissell's promises hollow, but she was also carrying his baby. It wasn't until she gave birth to their son, Chalmer Jr., that she decided to file charges.

Cissell had two choices: face felony charges of seduction or marry Ryner and have the charges automatically dismissed. He chose the latter and tied the knot on November 15. Bill and Bernice were together for the rest of their lives and had two more children, Charlene and Gary.

Heading into the 1928 season, Beavers president Tom Turner claimed that Cissell was "as great at shortstop as Hans Wagner, as great on the bases as Ty Cobb, and as great at the bat as Rogers Hornsby."

Once the regular season began, Cissell wasted no time proving that he could hit big league pitching, going 3-for-4 with a double and a run against Cleveland on Opening Day. He enjoyed a 14-game hitting streak and was hitting .366 on May 1, but couldn't maintain his pace and finished his first big league season at .260.

Cissell earned MVP votes and finished 15th in the balloting, and White Sox manager Lena Blackburne felt he could turn Cissell into one of the game's best shortstops. "Cissell is going to be one of the greatest baseball players yet. He is a natural." But the shortstop had a drinking problem that would plague him throughout his career.

"The White Sox paid a good chunk of gold for him as a rookie in 1928 and he should have been a great star, but he drank," wrote legendary reporter Red Smith years later. "He looked like a guy who couldn't miss. He had everything except the ability to take care of himself."

Cissell actually led the White Sox in games, at-bats, runs, hits and stolen bases, falling only two swipes short of the league's stolen base crown. He wasn't spectacular at the plate—no other batter in baseball made more outs—but he was fairly steady and consistent. In the field he led the league in putouts, tied for the league lead in assists, and finished third in double plays. And his arm was considered the strongest among AL shortstops.

The White Sox apparently remained unimpressed, however. Blackburne was fired after leading the team through a tumultuous season that included two fist fights with first baseman Art Shires and a seventh-place finish on the back of a then franchise-worst 59-93 record. With four games remaining in the 1929 season, Donie Bush was tabbed to lead the team in 1930. Cissell had once been described as a larger version of the diminutive Bush, but the new White Sox skipper had his eye on two new shortstop recruits and moved Cissell to second base.

Cissell came out of the gates like a man possessed in 1930, starting the season with a 12-game hitting streak, during which he batted a league-leading .431. But that proved to be his high-water mark of the season, as he batted only .246 the rest of the way to finish at .270, and made more errors than any other AL second sacker, had the worst fielding percentage, and finished second-to-last in assists, double plays, and putouts.

The 1931 season also proved to be a difficult one for Cissell; he suffered a knee injury that kept him incapacitated for more than a month and batted only .220. Bush resigned in October and Lew Fonseca was named manager, making him the fourth different major league skipper Cissell had played for in five years. Cissell took the offseason a little more seriously and reported to camp in the best shape of his life.

His renewed commitment appeared to pay off when he began the 1932 campaign with seven hits in his first five games, but he fell into his usual funk and his time with the White Sox came to an end when he was traded to the Cleveland Indians on April 24.

The move paid off and Cissell became a different player with Cleveland. "Cissell took over the job at second base where the Indians had been weak for several years," wrote one newspaper. "Not only did his hitting average soar...but he inspired the whole team with his fighting qualities." He batted .320 for Cleveland and .315 overall, and placed 11th in MVP voting.

Chalmer "Bill" Cissell.

But his success didn't last long. Cissell got off to a slow start in 1933 and it was all downhill from there, as he suffered through various injuries, a three-game suspension in mid-May for using profanity during an argument with home plate umpire Roy Van Graflan, and inconsistency at the plate.

He enjoyed a "power" surge in August when he smacked three of his six home runs, all coming in a six-game span in the middle of the month, but his season ended on September 15 when he underwent an appendectomy.

Less than a month after his surgery, Cissell was dealt to the Boston Red Sox. He spent only one year with them before being shipped back to Portland on February 1, 1935. The infielder had come full circle; after seven years in the big leagues, he was back with the team that had sold him for the record sum that scribes wouldn't let him forget. He enjoyed a very good year with Portland but his heart was still in the big leagues.

Cissell refused to play for Portland in 1936 and was shipped to the Baltimore Orioles of the International League. Before the 1936 regular season could get under way, yet another writer reminded his readers about the record price the White Sox paid for Cissell back in 1927.

"There was Bill Cissell out there playing shortstop for the Baltimore Orioles this afternoon, and it was not difficult to recall him as the most expensive piece of baseball bric-a-brac who ever came into the big leagues," wrote Shirley Povich in the *Washington Post*.

Cissell thrilled fans in Baltimore with his stellar play and batted .349 with career highs in homers (15) and slugging (.523), and was named the team's most valuable player. Philadelphia Athletics owner Connie Mack acquired Cissell in the Rule 5 draft and when Mack was asked why he'd take a chance on a player known for his appetite for alcohol, he replied, "I understand he only drinks at night now."

Cissell capped off his 1936 season by placing second in International League MVP balloting and carried that momentum over into 1937, getting off to a fast start for the Athletics, but on June 6 he was hitting .265 and playing subpar defense, and was sent back to Baltimore on June 11.

Cissell was a welcome sight back in Baltimore and batted a respectable .296 on the year. He followed with a solid .293 average in 1938 before being purchased by the New York Giants on August 1. Back in the big leagues, he struggled at the plate, batting .268 with an anemic .297 on-base percentage, but he enjoyed his best season in the field, posting a career-best .977 fielding percentage at second base.

Unfortunately, his 38-game cup of coffee with the Giants would be his last taste of the majors. On December 6, New York sold the soon-to-be 35-year-old infielder to the Hollywood Stars where he'd spend the next two seasons.

Cissell finished the year with subpar numbers, but was voted the team's MVP by the Hollywood fans. At 36 years old, Cissell entered spring training of 1940 as the second oldest member of the Stars, behind only new teammate Babe Herman who was 37.

He got off to another good start that year and was hitting .305 at the end of July, and he might have finished the season over .300 had he not been badly spiked in late August. Despite a heavily bandaged foot, Cissell refused to come out of the lineup and he finished the year at a solid .289. His glove work began to slip, however, and he finished last among PCL second basemen in fielding percentage.

Cissell was released and picked up by the San Francisco Seals two days later but didn't see much playing time and ended the 1941 season with a .247 average and only one extra-base hit in 40 games. At 37 years old, "Spider Bill" Cissell's professional career was over.

In 1942 he played semi-pro ball in California; In 1944 he was cutting beef for the Iowa Packing Company in Marshalltown, Iowa. Other reports had him working for the railroad. It was also around that time that Cissell's wife, Bernice, died.

In 1947 Cissell was offered a job by Dave Leahy, Comiskey Park's chief electrician. Besides working as an electrician at the stadium where he made his major league debut, Cissell also played semi-pro ball on Sundays.

His last hurrah as a ballplayer came in 1948 when he participated in an Old-Timers' game at Wrigley Field that also featured Rogers Hornsby, Freddy Lindstrom and Jim Thorpe. Cissell drove in the first run of the game, but the National League won, 5-4.

From there Cissell's life spiraled out of control. In December he was stricken with Buerger's disease, an inflammation and clotting of veins and arteries in the hands and feet, which made it impossible for him to walk without excruciating pain. He was living in a tiny one-room apartment in Chicago with his 13-year-old son Gary, who was supporting both of them with his $7-a-week grocery store job. In addition to the disease he was malnourished, resulting in a 60 lb. weight loss, and had hardening of the arteries.

"When my wife died I went to hell for a while," Cissell told Robert Cromie of the *Chicago Tribune* in January 1949. "In fact, I never did come all the way back. I used to drink too much. But if I can just get back on my feet again I'll be all right. But I'm just skin and bones now, must be down to 100 pounds."

Cissell ended up in Mercy Hospital but his prognosis looked promising and his condition improved in early February as the inflammation subsided.

Things were looking bright for Cissell as February turned to March. He had fully recovered and was ready to be discharged from the hospital, but he suffered a heart attack on March 5. He died on March 15 at the age of 45 and is buried at Mount Hope Cemetery in his home town of Perryville, Missouri.

PART II

CUPS OF COFFEE

Ed Conwell: No Luck for the Irish

On September 22, 1911, 21-year-old third baseman Ed "Irish" Conwell made his major league debut for the St. Louis Cardinals, taking over the hot corner in the top of the eighth inning with his team trailing Red Ames and the first-place New York Giants, 3–0. The game was of consequence to neither team—the Giants were well on their way to their third pennant of the modern era; the Cards were mired in fifth place, 17 games out of first.

But Cardinals manager Roger Bresnahan wasn't about to roll over for anybody and started bringing players off his bench in the seventh. Denney Wilie, a 20-year-old outfielder who batted .360 for Corpus Christi of the Southwest Texas League before making his major league debut on July 27, was called upon to pinch hit and promptly grounded out to begin the frame. Catcher Jack Bliss lined out to second and pitcher Roy Radebaugh fanned to end the inning.

Enter Conwell who took over at third base to start the eighth. Conwell had starred for the Portsmouth Cobblers of the Ohio State League, hitting .306 while committing only 14 errors in 140 games before getting his big break. Radebaugh retired the Giants in order in the eighth, then the Cardinals took advantage of some sloppy play in the bottom of the inning to cut the score to 3–1. The Giants went down easily again in the ninth and the Cards came to the plate down by two with one more shot to win or tie.

Conwell led off the inning and became Ames' seventh strike-out victim. Bliss singled, Ivey Wingo walked, and second baseman Miller Huggins singled to load the bases and knock Ames from the box in favor of southpaw Rube Marquard, who was en route to a 24–7 record on the season. Marquard had just beaten the Cardinals two days earlier on a complete-game four-hit shutout to earn his 22nd win on the year. In fact, in his previous four starts against the Cardinals, Marquard had allowed only 14 hits and two runs in 36 innings, throwing three shutouts, including a one-hitter on August 28. Needless to say, he had the Cards' number.

Bresnahan countered John McGraw's move by bringing in rookie outfielder Otto McIvor to pinch hit for centerfielder Rebel Oakes, but McIvor fanned for the second out and it looked like Marquard was going to save the game for Ames. But Ed Konetchy spoiled things for the Giants by doubling in the tying runs before Marquard could retire Rube Ellis for the final out. With the game tied 3–3, the teams moved into extra innings.

Bresnahan continued to rely on youngsters and brought in rookie hurler George Zackert who was making *his* major league debut after going 17–12 for Seattle of the Northwestern League. His big league career got off to a promising start when he struck out shortstop Art Fletcher for the first out of the inning. Then he coaxed catcher Chief Meyers to ground to Conwell at third for what should have been the second out, but Conwell booted the ball for an error. Marquard batted for himself and fanned, then Josh Devore doubled in Meyers to give the Giants a 4–3 lead. Zackert got out of the inning without further damage and the Cards stepped to the plate one last time with their backs to the wall.

St. Louis staged another rally when Steve Evans drew a leadoff walk, followed by an Arnold Hauser single that put runners on first and second with no outs. Conwell prepared to take his place in the batter's box with a chance to redeem himself, but Bresnahan was taking no chances and replaced the rookie with veteran infielder Mike Mowrey, who sacrificed the runners to second and third with a bunt to the left side. Bliss walked to load the bases, but Marquard retired pinch hitter Jim Clark, yet another rookie, and Huggins to end the game and earn his 23rd win of the season.

After only two major league innings, in which he struck out in his only at-bat and committed an error in his only chance in the field, Conwell witnessed the beginning *and* end of his major league career on the same day. He never set foot on a major league diamond again.

Conwell, a native of Chicago, began his professional career with the Class D Portsmouth Cobblers in 1909 at the age of 19 and made an immediate impression. "Red" Nelson of the rival Lima Cigarmakers told reporters that Conwell "had the most perfect position at the bat he ever saw," and predicted Conwell would become one of the Ohio State League's "most dangerous hitters." [1] And the *Portsmouth Daily Times* lauded Conwell for playing third base "splendidly."[2] Less than two weeks later, Conwell was already being touted as the "classiest third baseman in the league."[3]

He batted only .161 in 34 games but his fielding and potential were so great that Portsmouth management invited him back for the 1910 season. He wasted no time impressing the papers again when he got off to a hot start to lead the team in a handful of categories, batting .368 in his first 19 at-bats and accepting 24 chances without an error. But he couldn't keep pace and batted only .208 with a scant 16 extra-base hits in 131 games.

Regardless, Cobblers manager and second baseman Pete Childs remained high on Conwell and predicted big things for his third sacker in 1911. "He is one of the most promising players I ever saw and his hitting will improve because of the confidence he gained last season."[4] Childs could afford to be patient with his young third baseman; the Cobblers won the Ohio State League pennant in 1910 and Conwell was part of what *Sporting Life* magazine called the "stonewall infield," that also featured Childs, along with Ed Irwin at first and Wesley Hornung at shortstop.

Childs proved prescient. Conwell batted .306, led the team in hits and total bases, was second in triples, and stole 22 bases. In the field only one other third baseman in the league had a fielding percentage as high Conwell's .968.

His performance led to his aforementioned ill-fated major league debut, but he soon found himself back in Portsmouth where he would spend the next three seasons trying to claw his way back to the big leagues. He enjoyed another fine season in 1912, batting .292 and leading the team in at-bats, hits, doubles, and total bases. He also earned some extra money in August when he received a $50 check from the Bull Durham Tobacco Company for hitting the bull on one of their billboards during a game on July 30.[5]

It was the second time he had accomplished the feat, but he was far from being the only player in the Ohio State League to do so, prompting the *Portsmouth Daily Times* to issue an ill-advised recommendation.

"The ball players of the Ohio State League should smoke Bull Durham tobacco for the rest of their lives, for the company has been mighty good to them," wrote the paper. "Most of the players have driven out home runs, which entitles them to a coupon calling for a 75¢ carton of the famous tobacco. Several have walloped the bull, for which they always receive a check for $50."[6]

Later in August, *Sporting Life* reported that several Ohio State League players would most likely get drafted, including Conwell. Other potential draftees among the Cobblers were pitcher Lester Hartwig, shortstop Emmett Cain, and outfielder Homer Cain.[7]

But Conwell again manned third for Portsmouth in 1913 and improved his batting to .299, while finishing second on the team in hits and doubles, and third in total bases. His fielding went south, however, as he committed 33 errors for a team-worst .914 fielding percentage. He enjoyed a few thrills, though, collecting a hit and fielding flawlessly in a late September exhibition game against the Chicago Cubs on "Al Bridwell Day" in Portsmouth.

Bridwell, the Cubs' shortstop, was from nearby Friendship, Ohio but grew up and played ball in Portsmouth before making his major league debut with the Cincinnati Reds in 1905. He spent most of his career with the Boston Braves and New York Giants before joining the Cubs in 1913. The game attracted fewer fans than expected, but by all accounts, the day was a rousing success. The patrons who showed up were enthusiastic and the Cobblers put up a game fight, holding the Cubs scoreless for five innings before bowing to them by a score of 6–1. The Cubs' catcher proved to be none other than Roger Bresnahan, Conwell's former Cardinals manager, and the Hall of Fame backstop warmly greeted Conwell with a handshake when the latter stepped to the plate for the first time.[8]

But Conwell also experienced some setbacks. On October 25, the *Times* reported that he would have to undergo surgery to remove a growth in his left eye and that the obstruction had been bothering him for some time.[9] It wouldn't be the last time that Conwell would suffer serious health issues.

He recovered from the surgery, then went out and enjoyed his best season to date, batting .316 in 1914 with a career-high .389 slugging percentage. He also moved over to second base to make room for Eddie Goostree, who played third for the Cobblers for one year before moving on to the Rocky Mount Carolinians in the Class C Virginia League in 1915.

Conwell was rewarded for his efforts when he was drafted in November 1914 by the Waco Navigators of the Class B Texas League. The Cobblers also lost outfielder John Hickey to the draft after Hickey batted .316 and paced the club with 16 triples.

"Local fans, while pleased to see Conwell and Hickey go higher, will regret to part with their services," wrote the *Portsmouth Daily Times*. "For several years Conwell has been considered the best infielder in the Ohio State [League]."[10]

Conwell seemingly adapted well, batting .281 and belting his first two home runs of his career, but he lost his second base job and found himself on the bench in July. Navigators' manager Ellis Hardy had a change of heart later in the month, however, and

Freddy Parent

In the American League's first decade, Freddy Parent was one of the game's best defensive shortstops and a fair hitter. Not only was he the starting shortstop on the first World Series winner, the Boston Americans, but he was the oldest surviving player from that Fall Classic before he died on November 2, 1972 at the age of 96.

Parent's career doesn't stand out—he led the league in only one offensive category in his 12-year career (at-bats in 1902), and one defensive category (assists, also in 1902). But the man knew how to get the most out of each game. Case in point—he was part of six no-hitters and could have played in as many as nine had he not gotten his teams' only hits in three one-hitters.

Twice during his career he participated in two no-hitters in the same season (1904 and 1908), and in the latter year, the no-hitters were thrown less than two weeks apart.

He was Boston's starting shortstop when Cy Young tossed the first perfect game of the modern era on May 5, 1904; then again when Jesse Tannehill threw a no-hitter on August 17 of the same year. In fact, Parent made a play in the ninth that may have saved Tannehill's no-no. On September 27, 1905, Parent led off for Boston and had two putouts and an assist in Bill Dineen's no-hitter.

Perhaps Parent's most memorable contribution to a no-hitter came on September 20, 1908 when, while playing for the White Sox, the shortstop drove in the winning run in the bottom of the ninth while he was being intentionally walked to set up a force out. A's pitcher Eddie Plank threw one close enough to the plate that Parent was able to reach out and put the ball in play, allowing Frank Isbell to score from third on a bang-bang play at the plate.

Twelve days later, Parent was on the wrong end of a perfect game thrown by Cleveland's Addie Joss on October 2. Less than two years later, Parent and his crew were held hitless by Joss again on April 20, 1910. A little more than a year later, Parent played his final major league game on April 30, 1911.

started playing Conwell all around the infield. Conwell eventually settled in at shortstop and was considered the best shortstop in the league.

Conwell shifted back over to third base in 1916, but struggled at the plate, batting only .245 with an anemic .296 slugging percentage. Still, it was rumored in late June that the Cincinnati Reds had shown interest in Conwell and were on the verge of acquiring him.[11]

At the time of the report, the Reds were two games under .500, in fifth place, and their infield was a mess. Heinie Groh, who by the end of the decade was widely considered the National League's best third baseman, manned the hot corner, but five different men played second, led by Baldy Louden who batted only .219, and eight different men played shortstop.

Regardless, the call never came and Conwell remained in Waco. His slide continued in 1917 when he batted only .227 for the Navigators and saw his playing time reduced to 282 at-bats. Then he suffered through a terrible 1918 season when he batted only .205 in 12 games with the Fort Worth Panthers. He landed with the Evansville Evas of the Class B Three-Eye League in 1919 and rebounded nicely, batting .318 with a team-leading 149 hits. In the field, he paced all Three-Eye third basemen in fielding percentage at .937.

Again, Conwell's play attracted the interest of scouts and it was reported in late June that several from the Double-A American Association had their eyes on him thanks to his .350 batting average and fielding prowess.[12] But again, the rumors proved to be just that and he stayed with Evansville.

He didn't play in 1920 but rejoined Evansville for the 1921 season. Before he was able to get back in playing shape, however, the 31-year-old Conwell suffered a nervous breakdown and returned to his home in Chicago where he sought out the help of a specialist.[13] Then things turned from bad to worse when he became paralyzed in mid-August and was listed in critical condition. According to newspaper reports, Conwell's family didn't expect him to recover.[14] But less than two months later, he was in good health and moved from Chicago back to Portsmouth.[15]

His stay in Portsmouth didn't last long, however, as another undisclosed illness forced him back to his parents' home in Chicago in January 1922. Conwell lived in poor health until May 1, 1926 when he died in a Chicago hospital at the age of 36.

"Mr. Conwell played ball several years with local Ohio State League teams and in his day was one of the best third basemen in the minors leagues," wrote the *Portsmouth Daily Times* two days after his death. "He fielded his position gracefully and accurately and had an arm of steel. He also was a dependable hitter. Conwell came to Portsmouth from the sand lots in Columbus and, under the resourceful late Pete Childs, he developed into a corking good infielder right off the reel. He was quick to learn, had the faculty of diagnosing plays of the enemy and soon was considered the premier third sacker in the Ohio State League."[16]

Harry Lunte: From Chapman to Sewell

On August 16, 1920 the Cleveland Indians prepared to take the field against the New York Yankees to start a crucial three-game series at Yankee Stadium that pitted the first-place Indians against the third-place Yankees. Cleveland was a mere four percentage points ahead of the Chicago White Sox in the standings; New York stood within a half game and only 10 percentage points of first place. The Yankees, perennial also-rans over most of the franchises first two decades, had been strengthened greatly by the acquisitions of manager Miller Huggins in 1918, pitcher Carl Mays in 1919 and outfielder Babe Ruth in 1920, and were contending for their first American League pennant. The Indians were basically in the same boat, having finished higher than third place only once in their first 17 years in the league, before consecutive second place finishes in 1918 and 1919 put them among the junior circuit's elite.

Cleveland, helmed by center fielder Tris Speaker, boasted the league's best offense and second best pitching staff, led by 31-game winner Jim Bagby and Stan Coveleski, whose 2.49 ERA was second best in the loop. New York had the league's best pitching staff, led by 20-game winners Bob Shawkey and the aforementioned Mays, and 36-year-old Jack Quinn, who would go on to win 18 games. And only the Indians sported a more formidable offense than the Yankees.

Only a week before, the Indians held a 4 1/2 game edge over the Yankees and were five up on the White Sox, but Cleveland lost four straight to New York while the White Sox won five straight over Washington in the midst of a seven-game winning streak that cut into Cleveland's lead. Now the three clubs were separated by mere percentage points.

Mays took the mound for the Yankees; Coveleski toed the slab for the Indians. Cleveland catcher Steve O'Neill tagged Mays for a solo home run in the second inning to give the Indians a 1–0 lead. Two more Cleveland runs in the fourth bumped their cushion to 3–0, and that's where the score stood when popular and talented Indians shortstop Ray Chapman stepped into the batter's box to lead off the fifth. Mays, who employed an almost underhand delivery that *Baseball Magazine* opined "looked like a cross between an octopus and a bowler,"[1] threw a pitch that tailed into Chapman and slammed into his head with such force that Mays thought the Cleveland shortstop had hit the ball with his bat. While the Yankees hurler fielded the sphere and threw to first in an attempt to get the out, Chapman slumped to the ground in agony. He remained conscious and even had the strength to walk as far as second base before his knees finally gave out and he had to be carried the rest of the way to the clubhouse.

When play was restored, Harry Lunte, a little-used 27-year-old shortstop, entered the game to run for Chapman and became the answer to a trivia question. Chapman suffered a fractured skull that required emergency surgery and died the next day. Lunte became the Indians starting shortstop, not because he was the best candidate but because he was the only candidate. Except for Lunte, only outfielder Joe Evans had experience at shortstop but he was sick and had been ineffective as a middle infielder. Joe Sewell, who would eventually take over at shortstop for Cleveland, was stuck in New Orleans, held hostage by a manager who was refusing to let his prize player go until the Southern Association season ended on September 18. So the job was Lunte's.

Lunte had been drafted by Cleveland in September 1917, but with no chance to break into an infield that featured Bill Wambsganss at second, Chapman at short, and Larry Gardner at third, Lunte had to be content with his role as a reserve infielder. He made his debut on May 19, 1919 and went 0-for-1 as a pinch hitter.

The rest of the season went much the same. Lunte appeared in 26 games and hit .195. He had a reputation as an outstanding fielder and Speaker claimed that his reserve shortstop had the best pair of hands he'd ever seen, Nap Lajoie and Honus Wagner not withstanding.[2] But defensively his numbers were below average in 1919 and he boasted the worst range factor among American League shortstops. Speaker may have been enamored with Lunte's glove work, but

Harry Lunte.

he desperately sought a better hitter to replace him on the roster prior to the 1920 season. His search came up empty, however, and Lunte remained on the team, albeit in a limited role.

His chance to start finally came on August 18, 1920 in Cleveland's first game since Chapman was beaned. He went 0-for-4 in a game won by the Yankees in the bottom of the ninth when first baseman Wally Pipp blasted a two-run homer off Jim Bagby to give New York a rousing 4–3 victory.

The *Washington Post* reported, "The fans paid tribute to Chapman's memory by applauding Lunte his successor, when he first came to bat."[3] And so it went with each new stop on their road trip. Seventeen thousand spectators showed up at Fenway Park for an August 21 doubleheader to show their sympathies to the Indians and to applaud Lunte in a show of support. Senators fans did the same when the Indians played in Washington. When the Tribe finally returned home to Cleveland on September 3, Lunte received three standing ovations after making a handful of outstanding plays in a game against the Tigers.

Lunte's hitting continued to be anemic, but his defensive statistics finally matched his reputation as he turned in several spectacular plays and fielded the position as steadily as any American League shortstop, recording a fielding percentage of .979. Not even Everett Scott, the American League's premier defensive shortstop, could match Lunte's glove work that season.

On September 9, *The Sporting News* weighed in on Lunte:

"Cleveland fans have been following the work of Harry Lunte at short with great interest and have been gratified to see him come through in fine style. Of course, Harry is no Chapman with the stick and he doesn't fit into the infield combination as smoothly as Ray did, but he is a mighty clever fielder and manages to insert a base hit now and then. Lunte got a great reception when he stepped up to the plate for the first time Friday and responded with a sharp single, which went a long way toward establishing him in the good graces of the fans."[4]

By the time the article hit newsstands, however, Lunte was no longer Cleveland's starting shortstop. He suffered a pulled thigh muscle in the first game of a doubleheader on September 6 and had to be removed from the game. Although Joe Evans filled in admirably for Lunte, Speaker and the Indians front office knew they'd have a difficult time holding off the White Sox and Yankees without a legitimate shortstop anchoring their infield.

Despite Speaker's insistence that Joe Sewell wasn't ready for big league baseball, the Indians decided to give the youngster a shot.[5] Sewell had hit .289 and scored 58 runs in 92 games with the Pelicans and finished fourth in the league with a .938 fielding percentage. The 21-year-old was just as adamant as Speaker that he wasn't ready for the majors, but he was finally convinced that he was, indeed, talented enough to compete at the big league level and he boarded a train for Cleveland.[6]

As a starter, Lunte batted only .203 but fielded brilliantly, committing only two errors in 18 games. His fielding was so well respected that his absence from the lineup was met with much concern and Sewell's arrival did nothing to soothe those fears.

On September 16, *The Sporting News* wrote:

"Speaker put his highly touted new shortstop from New Orleans, Joe Sewell, in the game during Friday's contest, after Evans had performed disappointingly. Sewell is built along the line of Donie Bush but in what little he did Friday he did not exhibit the agility or sureness of the Detroit short fielder. In fact, after watching Sewell and Evans at short, we can only pray that Harry Lunte will recover rapidly from the charley horse he sprung in the morning game Labor Day."[7]

Sewell made his debut on September 10 with the Indians holding a one-game lead over the White Sox and a game and a half cushion over the Yankees. He played in the season's final 22 games and was atrocious in the field, committing 15 errors and fielding at an .884 clip. But he was fantastic at the plate, batting .329 with a .413 on base average. The Harry Lunte era in Cleveland was over.

Sewell helped lead Cleveland to its first American League championship, then was declared eligible to appear in the World Series against the Brooklyn Dodgers, whom the Indians defeated for its first World Series title. Lunte played sparingly in the Series, appearing as a defensive replacement for Wambsganss at second base in the bottom of the eighth of Game 2. That would be his last appearance in a major league uniform.

James Crusinberry wrote in the *Chicago Tribune* in late March that Lunte was Cleveland's best utility man prospect.[8] But when Wambsganss broke a bone in his arm in Spring Training, Lunte was penciled into the starting lineup at second base. Lunte was hitting the ball much better in the spring of 1921 than he had at any time in his professional career. John B. Sheridan attributed Lunte's success to his return to a free-swinging batting style that the infielder employed as a youth, but abandoned for a "choked-bat" style when he joined the Indians.[9] Apparently someone convinced Lunte that choking up on the bat would benefit him in the majors. After hitting only .196 in his first two seasons, however, Lunte went back to his old style and the difference was obvious. "I do not know how true all this may be," wrote Sheridan. "I know that Harry Lunte was one of the best natural hitters I have ever seen."[10]

Not long after, however, Lunte badly sprained his ankle while sliding into home plate during an exhibition game and was expected to miss the first six weeks of the season. The loss of both Wambsganss and Lunte forced the Indians to look elsewhere for a second baseman and for the second time in as many seasons Lunte was replaced by a player who would become a star. on April 11 it was reported that Cleveland had acquired Riggs Stephenson, the University of Alabama's star keystone man. With Stephenson and Sewell, both former Alabama stars, anchoring the middle of Cleveland's infield and Wambsganss soon to return, the Indians had little need for Lunte and finally consented to a deal with Sacramento in mid-May.

F. J. Powers announced the release of Lunte in *The Sporting News* on May 26, 1921:

"Lunte is one of the hard luck cases of baseball. One of the greatest fielders in the game, he was weak at the bat. Yet a regular job might have made him a good hitter had fortune favored him... Harry may yet find both his batting eye and some good fortune, which Cleveland fans hope he does, for he has always given the club his best efforts when called on."[11]

Lunte refused to report to Sacramento and it was speculated that Sacramento's owners would demand that Cleveland pay them $5,000 as compensation. But the Moreing brothers chose instead to hold Lunte's rights in hopes that he would report for the 1922 season. Meanwhile Lunte was demanding back pay for the 1921 season. Lunte finally agreed to report to Sacramento in February. When the former Indian finally arrived in California he told Lew Moreing that he didn't want to play on the west coast and promptly boarded a train back to St. Louis.[12] Moreing had had enough and suspended Lunte on April 6, then, sold him to Rochester of the International League a week later.[13]

Lunte reported to Rochester, but kept insisting that he be paid for the 1921 season. He filed a petition with Major League Baseball, but was denied payment by Commissioner Landis, who ruled that Lunte did not "present himself for work as agreed" and therefore was not entitled to any money.[14] Lunte's luck continued to work against him on the field as well. He suffered multiple charley horses in 1922, injured his knee and burst a blood vessel in his leg, all of which limited him to 116 games. Despite his continuous bad fortune, Lunte finished fourth among International League third basemen in fielding, posting a .965 average, and eighth among shortstops at .942.

For the first time in years, Lunte enjoyed an injury-free season in 1923 and responded by hitting .306 for Rochester and scoring 88 runs in 167 games. His fielding dropped off a bit as he finished 11th among third basemen with a .939 fielding percentage, but he was second in assists and third in putouts. He repeated his iron man feat in 1924 and played in every game for Rochester, hitting .289 and scoring 87 runs in 169 games and he led all International League third basemen in fielding with a .965 mark. After all the trouble he had staying healthy through his brief major league career, Lunte was the only player to play in every one of his team's games in both 1923 and '24 and he set a league record for games played in the latter. Apparently that wasn't good enough for Rochester.

Lunte learned through friends that Rochester management felt he played "indifferent baseball" in 1924, which had him considering quitting the team and playing independent ball around St. Louis.[15] "It will be recalled that Lunte fell into a slump in July," wrote *The Sporting News* in March 1925. "But the entire team went into a slump at that time and the Tribe lost four of five consecutive series right here on the home lot. Lunte can hardly be blamed for the losses of those games. He played much better ball than numerous other players on the field at that time."[16]

Lunte was given his starting job back, but he struggled at the plate and in the field, suffered a bit of bad luck when he was spiked on May 14, and lost his job not long after when Rochester purchased former Giants and Phillies third sacker "Goldie" Rapp from Toledo of the American Association. Through 56 games, Lunte was hitting .220 and was among the league's worst fielders, posting a .915 fielding percentage at third base and a .919 mark at shortstop, so he was sold to Atlanta of the Southern League on July 12. In typical fashion Lunte refused to report to Atlanta and was immediately suspended by Rochester manager George Stallings. Rochester attempted to sell him again in August, sending him to Mobile, but Lunte balked again and sat out the rest of the 1925 season.

He finally resurfaced with the Newark Bears in mid-July 1926, but he batted only .175 in 17 games and posted a pathetic .783 fielding percentage. His baseball career apparently came to an end following the 1926 season for he dropped completely off the radar after that.

Lunte died in his home town of St. Louis on July 27, 1965 at the age of 72.

Bert Shepard's Heroic Effort

After three seasons in the minors, pitcher Bert Shepard did what a lot of players did in the early 1940s—he went to war. A fighter pilot, Shepard was shot down over Germany in May 1944 while flying his 34th mission. His life was saved by a German military doctor (who turned out to be Austrian), who held off pitchfork-wielding farmers who wanted Shepard dead.

His right leg, though, was so mangled that it had to be amputated just below the knee, effectively ending his pitching career. Or so you'd think. A fellow prisoner of war fashioned an artificial leg for Shepard and the southpaw taught himself how to walk and pitch again.

He returned to the United States in February 1945, and six months later found himself on the mound for the Washington Senators. Facing the Boston Red Sox on the wrong side of a 14-2 blowout, Shepard was outstanding, allowing only one run on three hits in 5 1/3 innings.

It was to be his only major league appearance and he retired with a 1.69 ERA. On August 31 he received the Distinguished Flying Cross in a ceremony at Griffith Stadium.

Another interesting note about that game is that Shepard came in for Joe Cleary, who was also making his major league debut and who also never appeared in the majors again. Cleary owns two distinctions in major league history—he's the last native of Ireland to pitch in the majors (he was born in Cork, Ireland in 1918) and his career 189.00 ERA is the highest among pitchers who recorded at least one out.

John Paciorek: King for a Day

The names Mickey Mantle and John Paciorek sometimes collided in the same sentence. "I was the one destined for greatness and all that," Paciorek once said. "I even wanted to look like Mickey Mantle."[1] If the name Paciorek sounds familiar, it should—John's younger brother, Tom, played 18 years in the major leagues, was an American League All-Star in 1981, and finished his career with a .282 batting average in almost 1,400 games.

But John preceded him by seven years and made his major league debut with the Houston Colt .45's on September 29, 1963 at the tender age of 18. It was the final game of the regular season and Houston decided to play a lineup loaded with rookies, the lone exception being 25-year-old Bob Aspromonte, who had been Houston's starting third baseman since 1962.

The rest of the lineup read like a college roster—Glenn Vaughan, only 19, started at shortstop; Joe Morgan, who had just turned 20, was at second base; Jimmy Wynn (21) played left field; Rusty Staub (19) was at first; Ivan Murrell (20) was in center field; Paciorek (18) was in right field; John Bateman (22) was behind the plate; and 19-year-old Chris Zachary was on the mound.

Paciorek, at 6'2" and 200 pounds, was a powerful righthanded pull hitter who batted only .219 for Single A Modesto, but with 28 extra base hits in 78 games. "In batting practice I used to be proud that I could hit a thousand home runs foul," he once boasted.[2] Paciorek was suffering from a back injury and was in Houston to have it examined when he learned that the Colt .45's wanted to give their fans a glimpse of the team's future by sending a rookie squad onto the field to battle the hapless New York Mets. Paciorek was a big part of the team's future.

Having heard about other players being released for lesser reasons, Paciorek downplayed his back woes and jumped at the opportunity to play in the big leagues.[3] He had torn muscles in his upper back and learned he had "congenital malformations" that would impact the rest of his career.[4] "When they told me I had a chance to play in a major league game," he recounted to George Vescey, "I forgot all about the pain."[5]

Batting seventh, Paciorek drew a walk against Larry Bearnarth in his first at-bat and came around to score on a Bateman triple that also plated Aspromonte to give Houston a 2–0 lead. With his team down 4–2 in the fourth, Paciorek singled off Bearnarth and drove in Staub and Aspromonte to tie the score at 4—4, then came home on a sacrifice fly. In the bottom of the fifth, Paciorek rapped another RBI single, plating Aspromonte yet again, and then scored on another hit during a rally that would eventually lead to an 11–4 Houston advantage. In the bottom of the sixth, Paciorek walked against Grover Powell.

By this time, he'd been to the plate four times and had reached base via hit or walk in all four trips. He had also scored four times and driven in three runs in what would end up a 13–4 win for the Colt .45's. But he wasn't quite through; he had one more at-bat left and the Houston crowd gave him a standing ovation as he stepped to the plate in the bottom of the eighth. He rewarded them with his third hit of the game, a single to left.

"I don't know why, but everything seemed to slow down when I faced major league pitching," he recalled later.[6] "Everything went absolutely perfect for me. It was almost as if I was destined. Even when I walked I wound up scoring. And I made two nice catches in the outfield."[7] After one major league game John Paciorek was batting 1.000, slugging 1.000 and had an on-base percentage of 1.000. And he was perfect in the field, tracking down two fly balls for outs.

Alas, that was the beginning of the end. Paciorek was invited to spring training in 1964, but his back was still bothering him and his arm had become sore from overcompensation. "The fans would see this jerk running 100 miles per hour...but I had to do it. I had such a bad arm, I had to charge everything."[8]

He was sent back to the minors and hit only .135 in 49 games before back surgery ended his season and kept him out until 1966. He eventually realized that the comparisons to Mickey Mantle contributed to his downfall. "I wanted to look like Mantle so much that I was doing these crazy neck exercises to get the giant neck muscles that he had," Paciorek explained. "I was always working on my body. It wasn't until I went to college and studied kinesiology that I discovered I was doing bad things to myself."[9]

Paciorek spent four more seasons in the minors before hanging up his spikes in 1969 with a .209 career average. "Most people agreed I probably would have been a pretty good player," he told Jerome Holtzman in 1986. "I was kind of impressive at times. But I was always hurt."[10]

As of this writing, Paciorek is the only player in major league history with at least three hits to finish his career with a 1.000 batting average. "It's kind of a dubious honor," he said in 1991. "But I guess I'm immortalized. I did something no one else has ever done."[11]

Larry Yount: A Whiff of Coffee

Much like John Paciorek, Larry Yount had a world of potential ahead of him and an impressive track record of past success, but was also upstaged by a younger brother. In Larry's case his sibling was more than just a one-time All-Star; he was longtime Milwaukee Brewer and Hall of Famer, Robin Yount.

Larry was a Pony League All-Star who helped lead the Canoga Park/Woodland Hills California All-Star team to a second place finish at the Pony League World Series in 1963, then to the California Regionals in 1964.[1] Yount was the team's top relief pitcher.[2] One of his teammates was Rick Dempsey, who was drafted by the Minnesota Twins in the 15th round of the 1967 amateur draft and spent 24 years in the big leagues, most notably with the Baltimore Orioles, with whom he won the 1983 World Series Most Valuable Player Award.

In fact, six players from that team signed professional contracts. Bruce Davis was drafted by the California Angels in the fourth round of the 1967 draft; Terry Hankins was selected by the Atlanta Braves in the 11th round of the same draft; Arnold Murillo was chosen by the Braves in the second round of the 1968 draft; and the team's ace, Randy Cohen, signed a minor league contract with the Baltimore Orioles in 1968. Alas, only Dempsey and Yount made it to The Show. Well, sort of.

After starring for Taft High, Larry Yount was drafted by the Houston Astros in the fifth round of the 1968 draft. He didn't enjoy much success in '68, but was excellent in 1969 and '70 and earned a major league call-up in September 1971 after striking out a career-best 7.9 batters per nine innings in 22 starts for the Triple-A Oklahoma City 89ers.

On September 15 the Astros were 73–75, in fourth place and 10 games out of first when they hosted the Braves at the Astrodome. Future Hall of Famer Phil Niekro, in search of his 14th win of the season, took the mound for the Braves. Jack Billingham, who would later star for the Cincinnati Reds, got the start for the Astros.

Houston took a quick 1–0 lead in the bottom of the first, but Atlanta scored runs in the second, fourth and fifth innings, and led 4–1 going into the bottom of the fifth. Billingham lasted only five innings and surrendered all four runs, including Hank Aaron's 44th home run of the season in the fifth. Skip Guinn held the Braves scoreless through the eighth, then Yount got the call for the ninth. He was to face the top of the Braves' order—Felix Millan, Ralph Garr and Aaron—the latter two being among the best hitters in the National League.

But Yount never got the chance. While warming up in the bullpen, he felt intense pain in his right elbow. The *Los Angeles Times*' Steve Elling likened it to being stuck with a cattle prod.[3] Yount counted on adrenaline to make the pain go away. "Maybe I thought all that pain I had in the bullpen would change after a 30-second walk [to the mound]," he explained years later.[4] Yount was announced as the new pitcher and his name had already been entered into home plate umpire Ed Sudol's lineup card, but the pain followed him from the bullpen.

He tossed a couple warm-up pitches before calling a coach over and admitting he was hurt. "I shouldn't have even tried, but at 21, I would have bungee-jumped if they'd asked me," Yount told the *St. Louis Post-Dispatch*.[5] Jim Ray was called in to relieve Yount and allowed a single to Garr, but retired Millan, Aaron and Earl Williams to escape the ninth. The Astros plated a run in the bottom of the frame, but lost 4–2.

After a couple weeks of rest, the pain in Yount's elbow disappeared. But he never made it back to the big leagues. Control problems derailed his career. Suddenly he couldn't find the plate. "It was like an insidious virus," wrote Elling. "Coaches tinkered with his delivery. Teammates made suggestions. Between the lines, between the ears, Yount was an equal-opportunity mess."[6] Things got so bad he began seeing a psychiatrist. He continued to struggle before finally calling it quits when he was released by the Milwaukee Brewers in 1976. At only 26 he was washed up.

Larry Yount is the only major league pitcher in history to appear in only one major league game without actually facing a batter. Elling summed up Yount's career succinctly. "Some guys are in the big leagues for the proverbial cup of coffee. Yount had a teaspoon of espresso."[7]

PART III

PROBLEM CHILDREN

Punch Drunk: The Art Shires Story

Art Shires arrived on the major league scene in 1928 with much fanfare, almost all of it of his own making. The Italy, Texas native nicknamed himself "Art The Great" and once boasted that next to Babe Ruth, he was the biggest drawing card in the American League.[1] The cocky first baseman also came with a ton of baggage and a hair-trigger temper that hampered his career and landed him in hot water on and off the field.

Shires began his career in 1926 with Waco of the Texas League, and the 18-year-old was impressive. He was even better in 1927, batting .305, then enjoyed his finest season to date in 1928, batting .317 and committing only five errors in 105 games.

He so impressed the Chicago White Sox that they purchased his contract on July 31, 1928. Shires joined the White Sox in mid-August and on August 20 the *Chicago Tribune* announced that Shires, "the first basing sensation of the minors," would make his debut against the Boston Red Sox at Fenway Park.[2] He began his major league career with a bang, rapping out four hits against Hall of Famer Red Ruffing, including a triple in his first at-bat. So cocky was the 21-year-old that he boasted after the game, "So this is the great American League I've heard so much about? I'll hit .400!"[3]

He ended up batting .341 in his rookie season and was named team captain. For a franchise still reeling from the Black Sox scandal—the Sox had only two winning seasons since and finished no higher than fifth place in their eight previous campaigns—it was a curious decision, akin to giving Hal Chase the responsibility of stamping out gambling, or putting Babe Ruth in charge of curfew.

Shires drew immediate attention to himself. Two days after the first sacker's debut, sportswriter Frank Young named Shires a "keen contender for the crown as the tobacco chewing champion," which was held by Tigers catcher Pinky Hargrave. "Now there is considerable doubt as to leadership," wrote Young, "the cud which Shires masters being heavy enough to make him lean slightly toward the left side."[4] Umpire Tommy Connally took the hyperbole a step further and called Shires, "the chewingest player I've seen in forty years of baseball."[5]

Shires also had a taste for fine wardrobe and reportedly owned dozens of suits, hats, spats, tuxedos, and attire for golfing, horse riding, and yachting. John Kieran wrote about Shires, "He wore his fancy suitings and he sported his glittering canes. His haberdashery was chosen with infinite taste, rich but not gaudy."[6]

Legend has it that when Shires was traded to the Washington Senators in 1930, he reported to the clubhouse wearing a green jacket with pearl buttons, white trousers with green stripes, and a Roman candle necktie. When asked by a reporter if Shires was the best dressed player on the team, Al Schacht replied, "No, he's the *most* dressed."[7]

But Shires' natty attire couldn't contain the demons within, and he soon found himself in trouble, first with the law, then with the White Sox. On December 28, 1928 a 53-year-old Shreveport, Louisiana man named Walter Lawson died from an injury he suffered to his spinal cord at the base of his brain.[8] The man's death, though unfortunate, probably wouldn't have garnered much national attention, except that his injuries came when Shires angrily threw a baseball at a group of disapproving fans during a game between Waco and Shreveport on May 30. The ball hit Lawson in the head and he died seven months later. The fact that Lawson was a "Negro" made the incident even more controversial (although one can only imagine the public's "outrage" in 1928 had the roles been reversed).

Lawson's wife, Ida, sued Shires for $25,411, but Shires was exonerated by a grand jury on March 29, 1929.[8] The suit was dropped from the court's docket after an agreed upon judgment for $500.[9]

That was not the last of his troubles, however. Though he was considered one of baseball's future stars his off-the-field antics were becoming a problem. A day after being cleared by the grand jury in Lawson's death, Shires arrived at the team's spring training hotel long after curfew and so drunk that he walked right past White Sox manager Lena Blackburne without recognizing him. Blackburne immediately stripped Shires of his captaincy and warned that further infractions would result in a long suspension without pay and a $100 fine.[10]

White Sox owner Charles Comiskey ordered Shires back to his home in Texas until he was in playing condition.[11] Shires charged Blackburne with being "incompetent and tyrannical" and the Washington *Post* partially sided with Shires, placing much of the blame on Comiskey, who had gone through six different managers since the Black Sox scandal. "It may be that the White Sox have gotten the idea that a manager of their team is never more than a straw boss," wrote the Post.[12]

"Straw boss" or not, Blackburne vowed to "weed out the bad element" on the team. Westbrook Pegler reminded his readers that Comiskey had the power, as did all baseball magnates, to blacklist players, dooming them to a "state of suspended business animation, bound to a job, but forbidden to work at it."[13]

The recalcitrant first baseman remained on the roster, but was planted firmly on the bench while Bud Clancy played first base and played it well. Finally on May 15, everything came to a head.

Prior to that day's game against the Red Sox at Comiskey Park, Shires was admonished by Blackburne for wearing a red felt hat during batting practice; Blackburne felt Shires was trying to "burlesque the game" and wasn't taking his job seriously. Shires countered with a "number of large words not suited to household purposes" and threatened to run Blackburne out of his job. Blackburne suspended Shires on the spot and fined him $100.

Virgil Trucks

Virgil "Fire" Trucks had a very good 17-year career, winning 177 games and posting a 3.39 ERA in almost 2,700 innings, and he might have won 200 had he not missed two years due to WWII. Only twice did he finish a season with a losing record, but no year was more bizarre than 1952.

His first three starts were awful and he went 0–2 with a 15.95 ERA. His fourth start lowered his ERA to 8.47, but he allowed 13 more hits, giving him 30 hits allowed in only 15 2/3 innings through four starts.

In his fifth start he tossed a no-hitter against the Washington Senators, and his season improved markedly. From May 9 to June 29, Trucks lowered his ERA all the way down to 3.24. July didn't start well, but he came within one hit of his second no-hitter of the season on July 22 when he surrendered a lead-off single to Eddie Yost, then held Washington hitless the rest of the way.

Eight starts later on August 25, Trucks became only the third pitcher in big league history to throw two no-hitters in the same season when he held the Yankees without a hit at Yankee Stadium. He made seven more appearances on the year and his last start was a disaster, as he lasted only a third of an inning in an 11–6 loss to the Indians.

So what was so bizarre about Trucks' 1952 season? Despite his dominance in those three starts in which he allowed only one hit in 27 innings, he finished the year at only 5–19. Most of his problems were not of his doing—he received horrible run support as evidenced by the fact that he won those three fantastic contests by identical 1–0 scores. With just average run support, Trucks would have been close to a .500 pitcher (11–13).

So in his five wins, which included a complete game six-hitter (must have been an off night) and a two-hitter in 7 2/3 innings, Trucks allowed only 9 hits in 43 2/3 innings and posted a 0.21 ERA.

In his 19 losses, the Tigers scored only 2.7 runs on average, and in 10 of his first 13 starts, they scored more than two only once, averaging a pathetic 1.4.

Shires left the park, but returned before the end of the game to confront the White Sox manager. Words were exchanged before the two men came to blows, each landing a punch to the other's face before they were separated.[14]

The next day Blackburne declared that he was through with Shires and it was up to Comiskey to decide what to do with the first baseman.[15] Shires insisted he was through with baseball and planned to go back to school to get his law degree.[16]

Neither happened. Shires apologized and was reinstated less than two weeks after his fight with Blackburne. He finally made it into the starting lineup on June 4 and went 2-for-4 with a double and a run scored, but the White Sox lost to the Yankees, 4–2, dropping their record to 16–30. They were only at the quarter mark of the season but were already 17 ½ games behind the first-place Athletics. Although there was still plenty of time for Chicago to make up ground, they'd be lucky to finish north of seventh place.

Shires hit .312 and led the team with a .370 on-base percentage. Unfortunately he couldn't keep his temper in check and was suspended again in mid-September after getting into another fight with Blackburne in a Philadelphia hotel room. Blackburne was passing by Shires' room and heard a commotion, and when he peeked into the room, he found Shires using empty liquor bottles as "indian clubs and shouting for more liquor." Blackburne accused Shires of being drunk (again); Shires responded by knocking Blackburne down and bouncing his head off the floor repeatedly.[17]

Shires not only gave Blackburne a pretty good beating, but he turned his ire towards White Sox Traveling Secretary Lou Barbour as well when Barbour tried to intervene. Police took Shires into custody, but incredibly Blackburne and Barbour refused to press charges.

As far as Blackburne was concerned, however, Shires was persona non grata. "Shires is out, gone, through, busted forever. And I'm not kidding. He'll never get back into organized baseball after this." Shires countered. "Barbour and Blackburne walked into my room with their chests sticking out. Can you imagine those two stool pigeons trying to scare me? I just started swinging."[18]

Shires was suspended for the rest of the season, then did what only Art Shires had the audacity to do; he held out for more money, demanding $25,000 while insisting that he was as big a "drawing card" as anyone in the American League with the exception of Babe Ruth.[19]

Comiskey hadn't even reinstated him to the team yet, and was so taken aback by Shires' demands that he began calling him "Art the Peculiar" and the "Peculiar One." The Old Roman countered with an offer of $7,000, insisting Shires was lucky to be getting even that much.[20]

Shires eventually agreed to terms and signed for $7,500, far less than he was demanding, but slightly more than Comiskey wanted to pay.

But Comiskey was courting disaster by keeping Shires in a White Sox uniform. In the winter of 1929, Shires, buoyed by his pugilistic victories over the much smaller Blackburne, decided to try his hand at boxing. He enjoyed brief success, knocking out "Dangerous Dan" Daly in 21 seconds in front of the biggest fight crowd in the history of White City amusement park in Chicago (Daly was actually Jim Gerry, also identified as Jim Gary, a friend of Blackburne's from Columbus, Ohio), which earned him a fight against George Trafton, who played center for the Chicago Bears. Meanwhile, Shires demanded a bout with Cubs center fielder Hack Wilson, who had gained a reputation of his own for decisively settling arguments with his fists.

While Wilson was mulling over Shires' challenge, Trafton beat the "Great One" to a pulp and knocked him down three times in a fight that lasted only five rounds because neither man had the strength to continue. The fight was dubbed by one sportswriter as the "Laugh of the Century," while another scribe called it the "Battle of the Clowns."[21] Soon after, Wilson decided against fighting Shires because the White Sox first sacker had already been beaten and Wilson had nothing to gain by fighting a man with a tainted record.

Undaunted, Shires applied for a New York boxing license. But not long into his "career," he was suspended by the Michigan Boxing Commission after it was learned that his next scheduled opponent, "Battling" Criss, was offered money to "take a dive."[22] Only two days later, Gerry admitted that he, too, took a dive after being threatened that he'd be "taken for a ride" if he refused.[23] Shires was alleged to have been suspended in Illinois and New York as well, and one report had him suspended in as many as 32 states.

The boxing commission eventually cleared Shires after failing to find any evidence that he or anyone associated with him fixed his fights. But before Shires could step back into the ring, Commissioner Landis kayoed Shires' boxing career by issuing an ultimatum— "quit the prize ring or quit baseball."

Art Shires' boxing match with Hack Wilson was called off by Commissioner Landis.

In fact, he issued an edict that impacted all baseball players who considered following in Shires' footsteps: "Hereafter any person connected with any club in this organization who engages in professional boxing will be regarded by this office as having permanently retired from baseball. The two activities do not mix."[24]

Comiskey finally tired of Shires' act and sent him to Washington for southpaw Garland Braxton and catcher Bennie Tate on June 16, 1930. Shires was batting only .258 with little power, and the White Sox's catching situation was in such a shambles that the team would eventually use seven different men behind the plate that season.

Shires responded well to the trade although his arrogance preceded him. "I don't want this club to stand in awe of me," he told Senators skipper Walter Johnson. "Just call me Shires." He then explained that his troubles were over because Washington "appreciated his [alcohol] problem."[25]

"Gin is not good for an athlete," Shires explained. "Walter Johnson told me so. Did Lena Blackburne tell me so when I was with the White Sox? No. He just told me I couldn't drink it. He didn't appeal to my reason."[26]

Shires was terrific for the Senators, batting .369 and slugging a career-best .464 in 38 games, but despite a 94–60 record, Washington finished in second place, eight games behind Connie Mack's powerful Athletics. The Senators had three very good first basemen in Shires, 16-year veteran Joe Judge, and Joe Kuhel, whom the Senators purchased from Kansas City for $65,000. Judge was coming off one of his best seasons but would turn 37 early in the 1931 season; Shires had just turned 23 and Kuhel was only 24. Even if Judge stuck around for a couple more seasons, it looked like the first base job would eventually be inherited by either Shires or Kuhel.

But reports surfaced that Shires detested sitting on the bench behind Judge and "lost interest" in his work when he wasn't starting. There were also rumors that Shires had violated team training rules during the season and wasn't keeping himself in shape. Johnson was willing to overlook those things to keep Shires' bat in the lineup and tried Shires out in the outfield, but according to reports, he "failed to impress" in that capacity. His days in Washington were numbered.[27]

The offseason between 1930 and 1931 proved to be extremely busy for Shires and he appeared to love every minute of it. He was named to two major league All-Star teams, one of which played a series of games against the Negro League's Chicago American Giants in October 1930, and though the team included future Hall of Famers Harry Heilmann and Charlie Gehringer, the *Chicago Tribune* gave Art "Whataman" Shires top billing.

He was also slated to appear in films and married his bride, 18-year-old University of Wisconsin co-ed Elizabeth "Betty" Greenabaum on November 10.[28] A little more than two weeks later, the Senators sold the first baseman to the Milwaukee Brewers of the American Association for $10,000. Shires sealed his own fate during the 1930 season when he told Senators owner Clark Griffith that he was "too good a ballplayer to be sitting around on a major league bench."[29] Griffith apparently agreed and placed him on waivers. When every other major league team passed up on the opportunity to claim him, Griffith sent Shires to Milwaukee.

"Shires is the best ballplayer I have ever sent back to the minors," Griffith told reporters after the deal was struck."[30] Surprisingly, Shires was thrilled with the move, calling it "one of the greatest breaks" he ever got. "I won't be any trouble to anybody. I just want to play baseball and earn my back to the big show."[31]

Before he was to join the Brewers, though, Shires had plenty to keep him busy—in late November he was signed by Universal Studios to play opposite Kane Richmond in episodes nine and ten of "The Leather Pushers."[32] Then he took time to write a letter to Johnson, in which he called his former skipper, "the best manager and greatest fellow I ever played for."[33] He admitted that he didn't behave as he should have while sitting on the Senators' bench, and that he was going to take Johnson's advice and "hustle my way back to the big show."[34]

Shires got off to a hot start with Milwaukee and by mid-July major league teams began to show interest in him again—the Boston Braves, Cleveland Indians, Pittsburgh Pirates, and Philadelphia Phillies reportedly inquired about his services.[35] But the next few weeks came and went and Shires was still a Brewer.

Another month came and went and Milwaukee's price had dropped considerably. At the end of September when no major league team claimed him, Shires expressed disappointment that he might have to spend another season in the minors and seemed to recognize that his drinking and past transgressions made him undesirable to most big league clubs.

"I admit that I lifted a stein or two on occasion," he told reporters, "but I was always out there the next day to play or produce. I thought I was entitled to another shot in the big show, and I was disappointed when no one put in a bid for me."[36]

Finally the Boston Braves acquired Shires from Milwaukee for $10,000 and catcher Al Bool, who batted only .188 for the Braves in 1931 and boasted a career average of .237 in parts of three seasons. It was a far cry from the $100,000 and two players the Brewers had originally asked for.

A week later it was reported that a deal was in the works that would send Shires to the New York Giants for first baseman Bill Terry, who was in the midst of a contract holdout.[37] But Terry eventually signed and remained with the Giants (had that deal happened, it would have been a horrible trade for the Giants; Terry enjoyed his best season in 1932 and played four more seasons, batting .340 from 1932–1936 with three 200-hit seasons.)

Shires helped the Braves jump out to a 5–2 record in their first seven games in 1932 by hitting .370 in the season's first week. But things took a turn for the worse on April 22 when he suffered two injuries, the second of which knocked him out of action for almost a month. In the first inning of a game against Brooklyn, Dodgers outfielder Johnny Frederick smashed a grounder that took a wicked hop and hit Shires in the face, knocking him out and breaking his nose. Shires, no doubt used to taking shots to the face, stayed in the game. But in the ninth, he was knocked down for the count and wouldn't return until May 15. Joe Stripp laid down a bunt towards third baseman Fritz Knothe, who made a strong throw that beat the runner. But Shires was in Stripp's path and the two men collided head-on. Stripp was down for three or four minutes, but Shires had to be carried off the field and into the clubhouse. X-Rays later revealed a torn ligament in his left knee.[38]

Shires returned to the lineup on May 15 but wasn't the same hitter who'd started strong in April. As June unfolded into July and July into August, Braves skipper Bill McKechnie soured on Shires, who'd batted only .228 since his knee injury, and benched him. McKechnie accused Shires of the same things the Senators accused him of—"failure to keep in condition, and a lack of esprit de corps and whole-hearted diligence."[39]

McKechnie then tried to trade Shires to Chattanooga of the Southern Association, but Shires blocked the deal by producing a doctor's note that claimed he was out of condition, so McKechnie gave him his unconditional release. When Judge Fuchs learned of the release, he ordered it rescinded, and advised Shires to retire instead, offering to pay him his full salary while covering all medical expenses required to repair his knee.[40] Shires accepted the offer and underwent surgery on his knee on August 25.

With no job, a depleted bank account, and a bum knee, things began to look bleak for Shires. It would have been easy to feel sorry for him. In a candid interview with John Kieran, he revealed some information that made him out to be a somewhat sympathetic fig-ure. "From vaudeville, baseball, and fighting in the ring and one thing and another, I had $30,000 in cash at one time. Lost every nickel of it in a real estate venture...I had just $85 in the world left."[41]

In private, however, things were very different. Shires began to physically abuse his wife Betty, punching and slapping her in November. Not surprisingly, Art announced only two months later, in January 1933, that he and Betty had separated. He cited his frequent traveling for the rift and insisted that he and his wife were still friends.[42] Curiously, Betty refused to comment. But the world according to Shires was often volatile and muddled; two days later he announced that he and Betty had reconciled and the separation was off.[43]

Only a week before, Commissioner Landis had reinstated Shires from the voluntarily retired list. McKechnie announced that Shires would be given a second chance with the Braves, but that he'd have to beat out Baxter "Buck" Jordan for the first base job.[44] Shires had his work cut out for him—the 25-year-old Jordan tore up the International League, batting .357 and slugging .576, then hit .321 for the Braves. No one on the Braves hit better, and only Red Worthington and Wally Berger posted higher slugging percentages than the rookie first sacker.

Shires proved worthy of the challenge, at least early on, but when Fuchs offered Shires a reduced salary to serve as Jordan's backup in early April, Shires refused and left the team to see if he could catch on with a strong minor league or semi-pro club.[45] With almost anyone else, that might have been the end of the story, but with Shires, it was just the beginning. He was sold to Toronto of the International League, but balked at the move, announced that he would "never play minor league ball again," and began mulling over an offer of $25,000 a year to return to boxing.[46]

He appeared to be serious about the switch and even told German heavyweight Max Schmelling that he'd be ready to fight him within a few months.[47] Shires received a brief reprieve when Fuchs canceled the deal with Toronto and sold him to the St. Louis Cardinals instead. But Cardinals manager Gabby Street made it clear from the beginning that Shires was unwanted. "We don't need him. We have two first basemen now. He's probably to be sent to some other club."[48]

Sure enough, a week later the Cards sent Shires and three others to Columbus of the American Association for second baseman Burgess Whitehead. This time Shires accepted the deal, although he insisted the Cardinals had erred just as the Senators had. "The major leagues will realize once again, just as they did two years ago, that they made a mistake in waiving the great Shires out of the big show."[49]

Shires did well for Columbus, hitting .313 in 44 games, but again he couldn't keep himself out of trouble. On May 23 he was ordered by Judge Joseph Cordes to pay his former attorney, William Timlin, the $119.33 he owed him for defending Shires in a breach of contract suit.[50] Two days later, Shires was involved in a fight with a 32-year-old Louisville, Kentucky man named Jack Deacon, who broke his leg and suffered numerous lacerations when Shires picked him up and threw him down a staircase.[51] Shires was defending Louisville Colonels second baseman and former high school teammate Jimmy Adair, who started the fracas when he accused a woman of trying to "roll" him for $125. Deacon took exception to Adair's accusations; Shires stood up for Adair because he was a "small guy," and pitched Deacon down the stairs.[52]

Shires and Adair were charged with malicious assault and sued for $50,000. Deacon was charged with the same crime, as well as "conducting a disorderly house." Two others were charged with malicious assault, and one was charged with disorderly conduct. Deacon's attorney argued that his injuries were so severe that his leg may have to be amputated and that he could possibly die. The hospital where Deacon was laid up during the hearing claimed Deacon was in no immediate danger of either. Charges were eventually dismissed against everyone when Deacon decided not to pursue prosecution, but Shires was allegedly forced to pay Deacon's hospital bills.

Shires found himself in the news again on June 15 when American Association president Thomas J. Hickey barred Shires and three other members of the Columbus club from playing for the Red Birds for the rest of the season on the basis that they were being paid more than the maximum allowed by the league.[53] Columbus exceeded the monthly payroll of $6,500 agreed upon by members of the association and was fined $500. They also lost three of their best hitters and one of their better pitchers. Charlie Wilson was hitting .356 and slugging .575, Gordon Slade was hitting .353 and slugging .540, Shires was hitting .313 and slugging .477, and Jim Lindsey was 7–2 with a 3.69 ERA.

The Red Birds sat in first place with a 2 1/2 game lead over Indianapolis at the time of the decision. The decree had no effect on them, however, as they went on to finish 15 1/2 games ahead of the field en route to a pennant. In the wake of the Association's decision, Columbus traded Shires, Wilson, Lindsey, and pitcher Sheriff Blake to Rochester of the International League. Slade was recalled to the Cardinals.

The move to Rochester proved to be somewhat fortuitous as they also qualified for a pennant before losing to Buffalo in the playoffs. Shires batted .277 but was eventually replaced by future Hall of Famer Johnny Mize. He wouldn't stay in Rochester long. On November 16, 1933, Shires was dealt to Toledo. He wouldn't stay in Toledo long, either—he was sold to Fort Worth of the Texas League prior to the 1934 season. Not only was he no closer to rejoining the major leagues, but he was getting further away—Fort Worth wasn't affiliated with a major league team in 1934.

Jack McCarthy

Jack McCarthy was a fairly nondescript major leaguer who toiled for the Cincinnati Reds, Pittsburgh Pirates, Chicago Orphans (Cubs), Cleveland Blues/Bronchos/Naps (Indians), the Cubs again, then the Brooklyn Superbas (Dodgers) from 1893-1907. His best season was arguably 1901 when he hit .321 and fanned only eight times in 343 at-bats. But it was in 1905 that McCarthy made a mark in the record books that will never be erased.

On April 26, 1905 while playing center field for the Cubs, McCarthy started three double plays to set a record among outfielders. What made the feat even more unique is that all three runners on the back end of each DP were thrown out at the plate, something that had never happened before or since. McCarthy's assists were crucial as the Cubs nipped the Pirates, 2-1.

You'd think McCarthy was a double play machine but you'd be wrong. He started only one other double play all year, albeit in only 37 games, and only 27 in the other 1,046 games he played in the outfield in his 12 year career.

Shires spent a full season with Fort Worth, batted .287 and made 17 errors at first base after committing only three in 1933. With his baseball career flagging, Shires decided it was time to step back into the boxing ring. He was in desperate need of money and looking for any way to obtain it. He was matched up against Sid Hunter on January 31, 1935 and was knocked out in the second round.

Less than two weeks later, Shires fought a palooka named Joe Daley and knocked him out in the third round. It would prove to be Shires' final professional fight and he finished his career with a 5–2 record and five knockouts. Then the absurd happened—he was hired to manage the Harrisburg Senators of the New York-Pennsylvania

League at a salary of $3,500. He also played a little first base and batted a career-low .243. That was his last and only stint as a manager.

In 1936 Shires played semi-pro ball in Chicago for the Mills team, which also featured former major leaguer Hippo Vaughn. Shires played mostly in the outfield and batted over .600 but, according to Frank Finch of the *Los Angeles Times*, the Mills team released "Art The Great" because they didn't like that he was playing ball during the day and singing in cabarets at night. Shires then joined Bob Fothergill's Detroit team.[54]

In September 1936, some troubling news was made public when Shires' wife Betty filed for divorce and charged that Art had struck her again.[55] She cited "cruelty" as her reason for seeking the divorce. She and Shires had been separated for more than a year. The divorce was finalized on November 23.[56] From there, Shires' life deteriorated even further—he made money refereeing wrestling matches, then became a wrestler himself in 1937, but was virtually broke. When he was ordered to pay $5 a week to support his three-year-old son, he argued his own case. "When a man's slipping, people want to step on him," he lamented. "I'm trying to find work now, but, because of my knee, I can't play through a full season. For five nights I've slept in a chair, unable to pay for a hotel room."[57]

Though Shires was in the news on a regular basis, newspapers were printing "whatever happened to Art Shires?" stories on an equally regular basis. He signed with the Springfield Empires, another Chicago-area semi-pro team, and played with Hall of Fame pitcher Grover Cleveland Alexander, who was 50 at the time.[58]

Before his light dimmed completely, though, an article appeared in the *Hartford Courant*, linking Shires to Chicago gangster Al Capone, the most notorious mobster in American history. The article in question detailed a fairly innocuous incident in which Shires was photographed shaking Capone's hand at Comiskey Park before a White Sox game. When American League president Will Harridge saw the photo he was apoplectic and warned that players caught fraternizing with fans before a ballgame would be fined.[59]

But further investigation shows that the incident may not have been banal after all. When Commissioner Landis forbade Shires (and others) from boxing while he was still a major leaguer, it wasn't just because "boxing and baseball don't mix," it was also because Landis was aware of rumors that Capone and his men had a hand in the Shires-Trafton bout. It's not a stretch to believe Capone's thugs also fixed the fight against Jim Gerry and offered "Battling" Criss money to take a dive against Shires. At the time of Landis' decree, the Black Sox scandal was still less than a decade old; the last thing major league baseball needed was a fresh scandal involving fixed fights and gangsters.

After the July 1938 article about Capone, Shires received little press. He was mentioned sporadically in brief snippets of wrestling news, then more or less disappeared from the papers until May 18, 1948 when the *Chicago Tribune* reported that Shires, who operated a shrimp house and bar in Dallas, was running for a seat in the Texas House of Representatives.[60] He was confident that he'd get the support he'd need for a victory, but no one backed him and he was defeated.

He didn't stay out of the news long, though. On December 8, 1948 newspapers across the country greeted readers with disturbing news:

Shires Charged With Murder of Hi Erwin, Ex-Ball Player

Dallas, Tex., Dec. 7 (AP).—Art Shires, former major league first baseman, was charged with murder today in the death of W.H. (Hi) Erwin, 56, former professional baseball player.

Erwin died in a hospital here Saturday. Officers quoted Shires as saying he had a fight with Erwin October 3. Shires was questioned last night and released on a $5000 bond in a habeas corpus writ.

Shires and Erwin had been friends for 25 years. According to Shires he went to Erwin's cleaning and pressing shop to give him a steak, but things went horribly wrong. "He hit me across the face with a telephone receiver and I knocked him down without thinking," Shires told detectives. "I had to rough him up a good deal because he grabbed a knife and started whittling on my legs." According to the charges, Shires "willfully and with malice fore-thought killed William Hiram Erwin by beating him with his fists... and stomping him with his...feet."[61]

Erwin's physician reported that the victim died of internal injuries suffered in a fight. That's when police got involved. But Dr. P.A. Rogers, who treated Erwin after the fight, reported that Erwin died from hypostatic pneumonia and cirrhosis of the liver "with contributing causes being blows to the head, chest and abdomen."[62] A hearing revealed that Dr. E.E. Muirhead, who supervised Erwin's autopsy and conducted microscopic examination of the deceased's tissue, agreed with Rogers that Erwin died of cirrhosis of the liver and pneumonia.[63] Both testimonies would eventually work in Shires' favor.

Though the grand jury found that Shires "did inflict serious bodily injuries" to Erwin, the charge of murder was reduced to aggravated assault on January 31, 1949.[64] A little more than a year later on February 11, 1950, Shires was charged with simple assault and fined $25.[65] He had been involved in the deaths of two men in 20 years and got off with slaps on the wrist both times.

Curiously, six years later, the White Sox invited Shires to participate in an Old Timers' game at Yankee Stadium in August 1956; apparently they felt he could still pull a crowd, even in New York. The White Sox's roster boasted some fine ballplayers like Red Faber, Ed Walsh, Ray Schalk, Muddy Ruel, Jimmie Dykes, Johnny Mostil, and Bibb Falk. The Yankees loaded up with some all-time greats—Joe DiMaggio, Lefty Gomez, Bill Dickey, Home Run Baker—and All-Stars like Charlie Keller, Tommy Henrich, and Allie Reynolds, and won the game, 4–1. Shires spent some time in right field, but failed to record an official at-bat.

As the *Washington Post* put it once upon a time, Shires returned to "obscurity as a sports figure"[66] and wasn't heard from again until July 13, 1967 when he died from lung cancer at his home in Italy, Texas. He was 59.

Chris Brown: The Unfulfilled Career and Unsolved Death of the "Tin Man"

"[Chris Brown] could wake up in the middle of the night, rub the sleep out of his eyes, and hit a home run."—Michael Sokolove, The Ticket Out: Darryl Strawberry & the Boys of Crenshaw

Born in Jackson, Mississippi in 1961, Chris Brown starred for the Crenshaw High Cougars, a Los Angeles area team that also boasted Darryl Strawberry and four others who would be drafted by major league teams. After helping to lead the Cougars to the championship game in 1979 (Crenshaw lost to Granada Hills led by future NFL Hall of Fame quarterback John Elway) and being named Western League Player of the Year, Brown was selected by the San Francisco Giants in the second round of that year's amateur draft.

To that point in history, the only Crenshaw alum to be drafted higher was Ellis Valentine who went to the Montreal Expos with the 29th overall pick of the 1972 draft. A year after Brown was selected by the Giants, Strawberry became the highest selection from Crenshaw High when the New York Mets selected him first overall.

Some, including Crenshaw shortstop Fernando Becker, thought Brown was the better player. "Chris Brown definitely had more raw talent than Darryl," Becker told author Michael Sokolove. "Chris, by birth, could just do anything in any sport." But Brown had an attitude problem that would follow him to the majors. "You couldn't tell him nothing," said former high school teammate Nelson Whiting. "It was his way or he would cop an attitude like a little baby."

That would be a recurring theme throughout his career. A teammate's father tried to reason with Brown. "He had a hot temper," remembered Thedo Jones. "We'd talk baseball and I'd move the conversation around so that we talked about attitude—I was trying to settle the boy down, to the best of my ability."

Major League scout George Genovese likened Brown to Orlando Cepeda, but questioned his maturity. "He was strong like Cepeda and he could handle the bat," Genovese recalled. "I could find nothing wrong with him other than a little immaturity, which if he got past that...I figured he would be a superstar." Brown's own family called him "Baby," and his older brother told Bill Plaschke that Chris was a "mama's boy" who would "always hide behind [their mother's] skirts."

"He was a contradiction," his former high school coach Brooks Hurst said later. "He was the type competitor who would throw his body at the ball during a game but would not practice because of the slightest injury. He was intense and intelligent. The only problem was getting his head on straight."

Brown was only 17 when he began his professional career with Great Falls of the Pioneer League, and though he was fairly consistent in his six minor league campaigns before making his major league debut on September 3, 1984, his numbers didn't jump off the page and suggested he'd be nothing more than a solid defensive third baseman with pop in his bat. Unfortunately he was also consistently injured and never played more than 103 games in any minor league season.

Some of his "injuries" are legendary, such as the time he missed a game with the Triple A Phoenix Giants in 1984 because his eye was sore from "sleeping on it." And a media guide once listed a toothache as a "bruised tooth."

"He has a reputation for requiring motivation after periods of languid play in the minors," wrote The Scouting Report: 1985, "but he didn't show it in his first major league chance." In fact he was named the third baseman on the Topps All-Star Rookie team.

Only a year later The Scouting Report: 1986 claimed that Brown "was never able to gain the respect of his teammates for a job well done" because "his physical brittleness kept him out of 31 games and caused his teammates to point a collective finger in his direction [for the team's poor record]."

It could be argued that Brown was San Francisco's best hitter in 1985—he led the team in average, OPS and OPS+ and was money in the clutch, batting .344/.411/.479 in close and late situations, and .373/.448/.490 with two outs and runners in scoring position. But The Scouting Report: 1986 reported, "Giants management is going batty trying to discover what makes Brown tick and his woeful teammates often used him as an excuse for the entire club's troubles."

"The joke around the clubhouse last summer was that the pitching staff had more complete games than the third baseman," wrote Franz Lidz. Giants players had resorted to calling Brown "Tin Man" because he had no heart, and "Crystal" because he was so fragile. Catcher Bob Brenly claimed Brown "seemed unable or unwilling to play hurt and with pain." Infielder Mike Woodard took his criticism a step farther. "Sometimes he can be lovable, and other times he whines when he doesn't get his way and you feel like breaking his neck."

Brown insisted that critics had misperceived his gait as a lack of effort, and that he really was giving his all on the field. "To have people say I was dogging it was an injustice," he told Lidz. "I can do things and show no emotion and look like I'm not putting out. I walk around the field in slow motion. If I had an up-tempo kind of a walk, people would have never thought that."

After finishing fourth in National League Rookie of the Year balloting in 1985, Brown became an All-Star in 1986 when he batted .338 with seven homers and 35 runs batted in over the first half of the season. "He has been playing third as if auditioning for a highlight film," wrote Ivan Maisel in June 1986. He replaced Mike Schmidt in

Chris Brown's fast start in 1986 earned him a spot on the NL All Star Team.

the sixth inning and doubled against Charlie Hough in the bottom of the eighth before ending the game in the bottom of the ninth by hitting into a double play with the tying run at third base.

But that would prove to be the highlight of his season. After playing in 73 of the Giants' first 88 games, Brown appeared in only

43 of their final 74, and started in only 38 of them. His last home run came in San Francisco's final game before the All-Star break, and he failed to homer in his last 147 at-bats of the season. Reports in early September had him missing the rest of the season with an inflamed shoulder suffered in a collision with Cardinals catcher Mike Heath on July 4.

By then, Brown had already cemented his reputation as a malingerer and when he pulled himself from the starting lineup Giants manager Roger Craig, among others, was furious. General manager Al Rosen couldn't understand why Brown wasn't willing to play through the pain to try to win a batting title. Teammates and fans suspected that he was dogging it. "He comes out here today for batting practice and swings like he's Willie Mays," said one Giant player. "It's difficult to understand. The guy's got a chance for a batting title and for a pennant."

The Giants were in third place in the National League West, nine games behind the first-place Houston Astros, and Brown was their best hitter. He appeared to be vindicated—Rosen even admitted as much—when it was discovered that he had a partially detached bicep tendon that required surgery. In 1987, the Giants inked Brown to a one-year deal and he rewarded them with a strong April before a pitch from St. Louis' Danny Cox fractured his jaw on May 4 and put him on the disabled list. He missed 38 games before returning to the lineup on June 18 against the San Diego Padres. Two weeks later, he became a member of the Padres when the Giants traded Brown to San Diego in a deal that netted them Kevin Mitchell, who would win the NL MVP Award two years later, and pitchers Dave Dravecky and Craig Lefferts.

Even though Brown had been mired in a slump since coming off the disabled list, the Padres were hoping to get a cleanup hitter to bolster their lineup. "I know he's been having his problems, but he's a quality player, and maybe a change from that environment will get him hitting again," said Padre Manager Larry Bowa.

Hugh Bedient

On July 25, 1908 18-year-old Hugh Bedient fanned 42 batters in a 23-inning semipro game in Corry, Pennsylvania. Bedient, pitching for his hometown Falconer, New York team, faced 69 batters, allowed only six hits and fanned the aforementioned 42, including the last three of the game after his team broke a 1–1 tie and gave him a 3–1 lead.

In 1906 Bedient averaged 16 strikeouts a game while pitching for his high school team, then continued his success as a semipro until 1910 when he signed a contract with Fall River (MA) of the New England League.

He made his major league debut on April 26, 1912 and was one of three 20-game winners for the Boston Red Sox that season. Bedient allowed only 1 earned run in 18 World Series innings to help the Sox beat the New York Giants in eight games, and outdueled Christy Mathewson in Game 5 by tossing a three-hitter.

Bedient spent two more seasons in Boston before jumping to Buffalo of the Federal League in 1915. He made his final major league appearance on September 29, 1915 at the tender age of 25.

Bedient finished his career with a record of 59–53 and a 3.08 ERA. His high school and semipro strikeout abilities didn't translate to the majors—he fanned only four batters per nine innings, ranking 39th among pitchers from 1912 -1915 (minimum 500 innings pitched)—but no hurler before or since was better than Bedient on July 25, 1908.

But his struggles continued and it didn't take Brown long to take up residence in Bowa's doghouse. Nursing a sore wrist, Brown missed six games in late July. Following a 15-5 drubbing at the hands of the Cincinnati Reds, Bowa held a closed door meeting in which he questioned some of his players' desire to compete. "There are 20 of you guys who would go through a wall for me," he told them. "But there are three or four of you...you can get the hell out of here any time you want."

Bowa pulled Brown into his office and told him was tired of asking him to play, and that Brown would just have to come to him and let him know when he was ready. "I can't do any more with him," Bowa told reporters afterward. A teammate insisted on anonymity before tossing more fuel on the fire. "Yeah, we all know there are people dogging it. Everybody knows it. You can't fool the players. We're in here every day." The Boston Globe's Dan Shaughnessy reported that Bowa was already sick of Brown less than a month after he'd joined the Padres.

Brown's season ended on September 14 when his hand was broken by a pitch from former teammate Mike Krukow. He played in only 44 games for San Diego, the same number of games that Lefferts appeared in with San Francisco, and batted an anemic .232. The old joke about pitchers completing more games than Brown had almost come true.

Brown lost his arbitration case prior to the 1988 season and expressed displeasure with the way the Padres handled it, but also vowed to prove his worth by staying healthy and playing "between 147–158 games." He did neither. The season began badly and went downhill from there.

Bowa benched Brown after a three-strikeout performance in which he was brushed back by Krukow, then swung wildly at pitches out of the strike zone. Not long after, it was reported he was working on a new batting stance after starting the season with eight strikeouts in 14 at-bats. But Bowa did an about-face. After the skipper bypassed Brown for pinch-hitting duties in a 4–3 loss to the Dodgers, he announced that Brown would be his starting third baseman the rest of the way.

"We traded for Chris Brown and now we have to find out if that was a good deal for this organization," Bowa told reporters in mid-April. Fans must have been delighted; they'd been booing him since the first game and couldn't wait to heap on more abuse. Bowa had to pull Brown into his office for another closed door meeting, raising speculation that Brown could lose his job to Randy Ready who enjoyed a career year with the Padres in 1987.

Not long after, reports began to surface that the Padres were looking to trade Brown. The writing was on the wall when San Diego called highly regarded second base prospect Roberto Alomar to the majors, which would push Ready to third base. Brown was benched for about a week before he regained his familiar spot at the hot corner, then suffered his first injury, a painful cyst on his right hand, on May 10. A few days later he claimed to have tendinitis in his wrist.

Brown continued to miss games, which frustrated Bowa to no end. "'He has to tell me when he can play,' Bowa said for the umpteenth time since Brown joined the team from San Francisco last July 5," wrote Bill Plaschke. As if the baseball gods were conspiring against him, Brown was hit in the face with an errant relay throw in late May and was knocked to the ground. Although the ball hit him above the right eye, he was diagnosed with a bruised tooth root. Only in Chris Brown's world.

After leading the Padres to a dismal 16–30 record, Bowa was replaced by Jack McKeon, who immediately addressed Brown's injury history. "The guy is a legitimate All-Star third baseman when he plays," McKeon said. "If he has a legitimate hurt, fine. If the doctor says he can't play, fine. But if he can play, he's out there." To which Brown replied, "No comment."

Brown continued to miss games with injuries—he reinjured his hand after making a diving catch, jammed his shoulder, suffered a wrist injury after being hit by a pitch, either bruised his heel or twisted his ankle (depending on who you believe) while walking off the field, and bruised his thumb when he sucker punched teammate Marvell Wynne before a game against the Reds.

Between his injuries, his poor performance, Bowa's early-season ire and McKeon's eventual frustration, Brown managed to appear in only 80 games with the Padres in 1988, and only 70 as the starting third baseman. They were better without him in the lineup. McKeon turned the club around and led the Padres to a 83–78 record and third-place finish. Randy Ready and Tim Flannery started 88 games at the hot corner between them and outplayed Brown in every way. Needless to say Brown's days in San Diego were over and it didn't take long to show him the door.

On October 28 the Padres sent Brown and Keith Moreland to the Detroit Tigers for pitcher Walt Terrell. The trade hadn't even been consummated yet when arrows began to fly. "What kind of note is the malcontent Brown leaving on?" asked Bill Plaschke. "In the recently released Padre season recap of every player, his name is not even mentioned."

Brown had few supporters heading into the 1989 campaign and was taking shots from the media on an almost daily basis. "This might be the season that Chris Brown regains his status as a top-flight third baseman," wrote Robes Patton of the South Florida Sun-Sentinel. "Or, it might be the season that he reaffirms his status as a classic underachiever. Based on rumblings from San Francisco and San Diego, where he played the last four years, Brown was more mongrel than greyhound."

Detroit manager Sparky Anderson had high hopes, though. "I don't understand what reputation means. How he is with me and how I am with him, that's all that matters," Anderson said. Later he told Peter Gammons, "People are wrong about this guy. He's a great kid. He loves sports. You wait and see." To which Gammons responded, "Brown was so excited about playing for Sparky that he showed up [to spring training] 30 pounds overweight."

Anderson allegedly made Brown his pet project at the urging of his brother Bill who taught Brown at Crenshaw High and knew how to get the best out of him. Or so he thought. Brown couldn't escape his reputation for what "looked like a mystifying lack of resolve," and the press and former teammates continued to taunt him.

Dan Shaughnessy predicted Brown would disrupt the Detroit clubhouse and that Tom Brookens would eventually take over at third base once Brown broke down. Gammons wrote, "There is a pool amongst players and reporters to pick the date when Brookens gets his job back. No one has picked later than May 17." And former Giants teammate Mike LaCoss joked after being hit in the chest by a line drive and staying in the game, "Can you imagine if Chris Brown had been hit by that ball? They'd be performing open-heart surgery right now."

But Brookens was traded for a pitcher and Anderson gave Brown a half-hearted vote of confidence when he insisted, "He'll be my third baseman. There's no choice there. He's the man." Except Brown wasn't following Anderson's script, but rather a much more familiar one. On March 26, Bob Wolf of the Los Angeles Times reported that Brown had already missed five exhibition games with an aching back that had limited him to only 37 at-bats. "To those who have followed his career closely," he wrote, "the question is: What will be next?"

What was next was a strained left shoulder, suffered in his seventh game of the season while tagging Texas' Cecil Espy on a steal attempt. Except that Espy insisted Brown missed him. "He didn't hurt his shoulder tagging me because he never tagged me," Espy claimed. "That's a shame. All that talent. What do you have? A 230-pound stiff." Brown began the season hitting .174 with one extra-base hit and one run batted in, and whiffed seven times in 23 at-bats. He missed six games before returning on April 24, and raised his average to .195 before back spasms in late April put him on the shelf yet again.

Writers seemed to take pleasure in Brown's latest maladies. Mark Vancil of the Minneapolis Star Tribune started a "Chris Brown wimp vigil" and pointed out that Brown had missed 101 of 193 games over the past two years, but had never gone on the disabled list. Rick Hummel of the St. Louis Post-Dispatch wrote, "Oft-injured third baseman Chris Brown reached the 162-game mark—for his last two full years."

Finally on May 19 everything came to a head and Brown's major league career was over. With the Tigers mired in sixth place and reeling from a 14–24 record, Detroit management sent Sparky Anderson home to California to recover from exhaustion, and they released Brown who was hitting .193 with no home runs and four RBIs in 17 games.

Tigers General Manager Bill Lajoie cited "insufficient skill" as his reason for waiving Brown. Anderson told reporters, "I've never ripped a player in 20 years but. . ." before a cooler head stopped him from finishing his sentence. And Tigers coach Dick Tracewski, who served as interim manager in Anderson's absence, piled on. "We knew he was going to be a problem from the first week of spring training," he said. "He'd sit there and watch cartoons by the hour, and you'd just wonder what was going on in his head."

Brown was confused and upset. "They said I didn't want to play," he said. "How could I not want to play? If it had been Alan Trammell, would they have doubted he was really hurt?"

Critics came out of the woodwork to malign Brown, including his former high school and All-Star teammate Darryl Strawberry who reflected on the trade that sent Brown to San Diego for Kevin Mitchell in 1987. "Both got offered lots of advice and encouragement along the way," he said of Mitchell and Brown. "The difference was that Kevin listened. With Chris, advice went in one ear and kept right on going." About that same trade, one unnamed Giants official said, "We'd heard Mitchell wanted to play every day. We got him for a guy who didn't."

Larry Bowa praised Brown's talent while criticizing his desire—"I've seen Chris do things in the field that would make your head spin," he told Sports Illustrated. "He'd make great plays. He'd hit balls 500 feet. Then he'd show up the next day and say he was too hurt to play."

Brown was signed by the Pittsburgh Pirates and assigned to Triple A Buffalo, much to the dismay of Pirates skipper Jim Leyland who wanted nothing to do with him. The third sacker flourished, hitting .343 with five homers and 32 RBIs in 57 games, but continued to confound everyone around him. "He gets something going, then he's injured for two days," said Pirates GM Larry Doughty in August. "All these freaky things happen to him. He's had six or seven minor things happen already." Doughty admitted that Brown's chances of being with Pittsburgh in September were practically non-existent.

And that the Pirates' third baseman was 26-year-old two-time All-Star Bobby Bonilla provided a contrast that made Brown look all the more fragile and apathetic. Bonilla led the National League in games played with 163 (the Pirates had two rainouts that resulted in ties and played 164 games in 1989), was second in plate appearances and third in at-bats. That year, Bonilla had more plate appearances and at-bats than Brown had compiled in his last three years in the majors.

Brown never appeared with the Pirates and signed a minor league contract with the Cincinnati Reds, who believed him when he said he was ready to go back to the majors. Word was that boyhood friend Eric Davis convinced the Reds to sign Brown as a favor, but manager Lou Piniella denied those reports. And Brown said all the right things, and in the third person to boot. "If Chris Brown has to go out and play 162 games with a broken arm this season just to prove he can do it, that's what it's going to take," he said.

Of course, Brown had sung that same tune before and had yet to prove he could play more than 80 games, let alone twice that. He'd never get the chance, though. He was released in late March.

He played for the Monterrey Sultanes in the Mexican League in 1993 and tried to come back to the majors as a replacement player in 1995, but went 0 for 7 with Triple A Indianapolis in three games before calling it a career.

Brown's first couple years out of baseball were spent taking care of his daughter, Paris, while his wife Lisa worked as a flight attendant for Continental Airlines. Then he landed a job in construction and suffered neck and back injuries when the dump truck he was driving slid off a hill in Los Angeles. Later he worked in the Houston area, operating an 18-story high crane. It was a life that Sokolove claimed "suits [Brown] far better than big-league ball ever did. It turns out he was much better at getting up at dawn, earning an hourly wage, and being a family man than he ever was at traveling the National League circuit and playing baseball."

But his world began to unravel. He was laid off from his job, forcing him to seek employment in the most dangerous of conditions—war-torn Iraq, where he drove a diesel truck for Halliburton. "It's a place I would've never thought 20 years ago that I'd be," Brown told the press. During his time in Iraq, Brown had some close calls; he once narrowly avoided a gunman's bullet that struck his windshield, and he was a short distance away from an attack that claimed the lives of six Halliburton employees and a soldier, and found one driver kidnapped. "I believe God has a plan for me," said Brown. "Regardless of where I am, I figure the Lord will come get me. I might as well be making good money."

After three tours in Iraq, Brown came home to a shattered life that included a divorce, foreclosure on his home in Sugar Land, Texas, and a probable case of Post-Traumatic Stress Disorder. "Neighbors...said Brown seemed traumatized by his experiences in

Iraq," wrote the Los Angeles Times, "and that there was friction between Brown and his wife." Lisa moved out of the house and took Paris with her. Brown was having financial difficulties despite making very good money working for Halliburton, and Wells Fargo began foreclosing on their home.

That's when things turned bizarre. In the early morning hours of November 30, 2006, flames swept through Brown's house while, unbeknownst to authorities, he was inside. When firefighters arrived, the house was fully engulfed.

"The house was vacant when our firefighters arrived," claimed Doug Adolph of the Sugar Land Fire Department. "There was no one there, and we confirmed with neighbors that the house had been vacant for some time." Except it wasn't. Brown sustained massive injuries, so much so that police were unable to question him due to his condition. Yet he was able to explain what happened to his family—he had been abducted by burglars who tied him up and set his house on fire while he was still inside. Amazingly, Brown was able to escape with his life and somehow made it to a hospital nine miles away.

Investigators didn't believe Brown's story. "They declined to discuss whether Brown was the primary suspect in the arson investigation but made clear that the version of events they culled together from interviewing neighbors and firefighters at the scene was different from the one Brown shared with family members," reported the LA Times.

After a nearly month-long stay in the intensive care unit, Brown died on December 26, 2006. He was only 45 years old.

Gone Fishin': The Sobering Case of "Shufflin' Phil" Douglas

When "Shufflin' Phil" Douglas arrived on the baseball scene in 1910 at the tender age of 20 he brought with him size and a fastball impressive enough to draw comparisons to Walter Johnson.[1] Douglas, a product of Cedartown, Georgia, was a big man, especially for that era, standing 6' 3" and weighing 190 pounds, who threw especially hard. Eventually he would boast four pitches in his repertoire—spitball, curve, fastball, and change-up—though he relied mostly on a devastating spitter that he learned from Hall of Famer Ed Walsh in 1912.[2]

His first full season in organized ball was in 1911 when he led the Class C Macon Peaches with a 28–11 record, which so impressed the Chicago White Sox that they purchased his contract. He began the 1912 season with Des Moines of the Class A Western League before joining the White Sox and making his first major league start on August 30. He went seven innings against Cleveland in a 7–2 loss that also marked the debut of ill-fated Indians shortstop Ray Chapman.

Douglas appeared in two more games the rest of the way and went to spring training with the White Sox in 1913. He did "exceptionally well," but was shipped to the San Francisco Seals of the Pacific Coast League, then went 10–10 with Spokane of the Class B Northwestern League, a team that featured future Hall of Fame hurler Stan Coveleski and Black Sox co-conspirator Swede Risberg.[3] Douglas was acquired by the Cincinnati Reds in the 1913 draft and earned a spot in the Reds' rotation in 1914.

Cincinnati finished in last place that year, 34 1/2 games behind the eventual champion "Miracle Braves" of Boston, but Douglas

Phil Douglas, the source of much
frustration for manager
John McGraw.

enjoyed a very good season despite a record of only 11-18. He led the team in a handful of categories, including ERA at 2.56, and finished among the top ten in the National League in three of them. He also incurred his first fine when Reds manager Buck Herzog docked him $100 for violating training rules. Douglas had come from a hard-drinking southern family and developed a taste for alcohol in his late teens. He was also used to a more relaxed lifestyle than the one he found in organized baseball.

"The sacrifice of his fishing and drinking days between starts was a big one for Phil Douglas," wrote Tom Clark, author of One Last Round for the Shuffler, "and one which, for all his love of baseball, he was not always willing to make."[4]

The spitballer was awful for Cincinnati in 1915 and was suspended briefly in early May for "tanking up."[5] Tired of Douglas' act, the Reds sold him to the Brooklyn Robins on June 14 for $10,000.

Brooklyn was taking a huge risk; despite his slow start, there was no questioning Douglas' abilities, but his commitment to the game was secondary to his craving for hard liquor, which made it impossible for him to remain subordinate to his employers. The suspension in May was one of three times he "broke training" with the Reds before he was sold to Brooklyn. Brooklyn manager Wilbert Robinson thought that if he could keep Douglas sober, he'd have the best pitcher in the NL. But that was easier said than done. "Drinking was not a habit with Douglas—it was a disease," wrote Harry A. Williams.[6]

Douglas regained his form with Brooklyn, going 5–5 with a solid 2.62 ERA in 20 games, but was with the team only a month before being suspended by Robinson for suffering from "dizzy spells."[7] The suspension didn't last long; Douglas was on the hill to face the Pittsburgh Pirates only two days later. But he continued to violate the team's training rules and was waived by Brooklyn in early September. The Cubs and Braves both placed a claim on Douglas before NL president John Tener awarded him to Chicago.

He started four games for the Cubs and was fantastic, but he quickly wore out his welcome and they began shopping him during the offseason. No deal was made, however, and Douglas stayed with the Cubs.

He brought more trouble on himself in 1916 when skipper Joe Tinker smelled alcohol on his enigmatic hurler at the team's hotel in Tampa Bay during spring training and suspended Douglas indefinitely. Douglas claimed the odor emanating from his body was actually garlic from a Spanish restaurant he'd recently frequented.

"Honest, Joe, I haven't had a drop for three months," Douglas lied. "That garlic that you get in these Spanish dumps certainly sticks to a fellow." Tinker kicked him out of the hotel and insisted that Douglas would never pitch for the Cubs again. "He's through. I won't have him on my ball club and I won't have him where my ball club is."[8]

Douglas disappeared and was reportedly heading for Cowan, Tennessee when Tinker received a telegram from Mike Kelley of the St. Paul Saints of the American Association in which he offered to assume Douglas' contract. The Cubs sold Douglas to St. Paul and he won 12 games for them. It would be his last minor league stint.[9]

After leading the Cubs to a 67–86 record and fifth-place finish, Tinker was replaced by Braves coach Fred Mitchell prior to the 1917 campaign. Douglas was given a fresh start and he made the most of it, tossing a four-hit shutout in a 2–0 victory over Pittsburgh in his first start, then earned a 9–2 complete-game victory over the Cardinals on April 18. Sporting Life magazine predicted Douglas would be Mitchell's "principal winner," but only if he saw the "error of his ways" and "concentrated on baseball."[10]

"Douglass [sic] would rank among the first five pitchers every year were he to take care of himself," wrote the mag. "His ability is unquestioned."[11] Douglas wasn't Mitchell's principal winner that year—Hippo Vaughn won 23 games to Douglas' 14—but he was second on the staff in victories, posted a very good 2.55 ERA, and finished among NL leaders in eight different categories, while pacing the senior circuit in games with 51.

For the most part Douglas stayed out of trouble that year. J.C. Kofoed of Baseball Magazine suggested, "If the big southerner had taken care of himself a few years back he might have rated with [Grover Cleveland] Alexander today."[12] It was an ironic comparison considering Alexander would become one of the more celebrated alcoholics the game has ever known.

Prior to the 1918 season, J.V. Fitz Gerald of the Washington Post gave Cubs fans a reason to be optimistic when he called the Cubs' rotation the best in the National League and possibly the equal of the Red Sox's staff, led by Babe Ruth and Carl Mays.[13] Chicago had added Alexander in a trade with the Phillies, and they had Vaughn, Lefty Tyler, Claude Hendrix and Douglas to round out the rotation.

Even without Alexander for most of the year and only a half-season's worth of Douglas, who suffered an attack of appendicitis in February and wasn't able to make his first start of the season until June 6, the Cubs finished the 1918 season with the best record in baseball at 84–45 and a World Series berth against the Red Sox. They also made Fitz Gerald look downright prescient by posting a 2.18 ERA, best in the National League and 13 points better than the Red Sox's 2.31.

Douglas finished with 10 wins and posted a then career-best 2.13 ERA, but the only action he saw in the Fall Classic came in Game 4 when he relieved Tyler in the eighth inning and took the loss when he allowed an unearned run on a single, a passed ball, and his own throwing error to first base. The Sox defeated the Cubs in six games for their fifth championship in 18 years.

The Cubs were expected to repeat as NL champions in 1919 and Douglas did his part, going 10–6 with a 2.00 ERA in 25 appearances. But through 80 games, Chicago was languishing in third place, nine games behind the first-place New York Giants. The Giants were looking to add pitching depth and needed to unload outfielder Dave Robertson, who had refused to play for John McGraw, so on July 25 the Giants sent Robertson to Chicago for Douglas. When asked why he was so willing to part with Douglas, Mitchell told writers, "I never knew where the hell he was, or whether he was fit to work."[14]

McGraw wasn't particularly worried about Douglas' history, though. "I know I am getting myself in for something when I take on Douglas," he told the writers, "but I am sure I can handle him."[15]

On the field, Douglas did, in fact, prove to be a valuable addition. He posted a 2.10 ERA, sported the best strikeout per nine innings mark among the starters, and had the best K/BB ratio by far. But Douglas' demons began to get the best of him again and his behavior became erratic as the pennant race heated up. He won his first two games with the Giants, but the Reds caught New York on July 30 and passed them a day later. From August 5 to August 19, he lost his last four starts and that sent him over the edge.

Douglas went AWOL and disappeared for a few days, prompting McGraw to suspend him indefinitely for leaving the team without permission.[16] Sportswriter Hugh Fullerton reported three days later that Douglas insisted that a member of the Reds had drugged his lemonade and put him out of commission. It was a farcical claim, but Fullerton regaled his readers with a plethora of tales about past

Iron Davis

George Allen "Iron" Davis won only eight games in his professional career and once went 1–16 for the Jersey City Skeeters in 1913. In fact, he boasted a career record of 2–21 in both the majors and minors heading into a start

"Iron" Davis.

against the Philadelphia Phillies on September 9, 1914.

That day the spitballer packed nearly his entire career's success into one game when he no-hit the Phillies for his second big league victory, and only the third of his professional career. Davis went 3–3 for the Braves in 1914, and again in 1915, then went 0–2 for Providence in 1916, finishing his professional career with a record of 8–28.

Davis was more successful off the field. After retiring, he obtained a law degree from Harvard, and practiced law and taught astronomy in Buffalo, NY, not far from his birthplace of Lancaster, NY.

druggings, poisonings, and nefarious plots that allegedly impacted previous pennant races.[17]

The truth was that Douglas couldn't stand McGraw and didn't like New York, so he went back to Chicago and signed on to pitch for the Logan Squares, a semi-pro team.[18] Douglas appeared to have a change of heart, though, and McGraw sent word that the incident was closed and that Douglas could return to the team. The manager reportedly refunded the fines he'd imposed on the pitcher. But Douglas opted to remain in Chicago instead.[19]

As one would expect, Douglas dominated the lesser semi-pro batters and allowed only two runs in 49 innings. But he apparently tired of facing inferior competition and applied for reinstatement in January 1920. The National Commission approved his application but warned him that future transgressions would result in a heavy fine.[20] Fitz Gerald called the warning nothing more than a "verbal spanking," and asserted that Douglas' disappearance was an "out and out case of desertion." But he speculated that McGraw was willing to take Douglas back merely to use him as trade bait during the offseason.[21]

McGraw had other plans, however, and kept Douglas on the team. He hired detectives to follow Douglas and keep an eye on his every move. The pitcher resented the intrusion into his personal life, but he pitched well, tying his season-best in wins with 14 and posting a solid 2.71 ERA. Despite being bird-dogged everywhere he went, Douglas occasionally managed to elude detectives long enough to get himself into trouble. On July 9, McGraw suspended Douglas again for "failure to keep in condition."[22] The Giants were in Chicago for a four-game series with the Cubs and Douglas fell off the wagon on the first day. He last pitched on July 2 and wouldn't appear again until July 17.

Word was that opposing teams would tempt Douglas with liquor prior to games he was scheduled to pitch. "When right, Douglas is the best right-hander in the National League today, and when wrong he is all wrong," wrote Harry A. Williams. "However that may be, when Shuffling Phillip skids it's a long skid with a loud crash at the other end."[23]

McGraw became so fed up with his recalcitrant hurler and his ineffective detectives that he hired a man named "Shorty" O'Brien to keep tabs on Douglas. The pair drew stares everywhere they went—O'Brien stood only 5' 1" tall; Douglas was 6' 3". McGraw allegedly offered Douglas a bonus of between $3,000–3,500 if he stayed sober during the season, and O'Brien was brought in to help him do it. Instead of balking at the idea of having a "keeper" whose sole purpose was to keep him out of trouble, Douglas hit it off with O'Brien and they became friends.[24]

Douglas made it through the rest of the 1920 season with no more infractions, but McGraw had had enough and placed him on the trading block in November. But again Douglas remained with the team, and again McGraw would be forced to deal with one of Douglas' "vacations" during the 1921 season.

Douglas had gotten off to a good start, but McGraw's decision to leave him in for the full nine innings against the Phillies on June 27 prompted him to abandon the Giants again. Philadelphia tagged Douglas for 12 runs on 19 hits, five of which were homers, in a 12–8 victory that increased his ERA more than a full run from 3.84 to 4.86.

Despite yet another defection, McGraw reinstated the troubled hurler only four days later.[25] Douglas went only 9–7 the rest of the way and posted his worst ERA of his career at 4.22, but he kept his nose clean over the second half of the season, won a career-best 15 games, and led the league in shutouts.

More importantly, "The Shuffler" was fantastic in the World Series against the Yankees, going 2–1 with a 2.08 ERA and fanning 17 batters in 26 innings to help lead the Giants to their first World Series title since 1905. McGraw called Douglas' performance, "among the best pitching that has ever been displayed in a World Series."[26] And Babe Ruth allegedly told Douglas that he was "as tough a man as I've seen in [the American League]."[27]

But that wasn't enough to keep him off the trading block for yet another offseason. In late February 1922 the New York Times reported that Douglas was on the market again. McGraw refused to call him a contract holdout, but it was speculated that he was trying to trade him for that very reason.[28]

But there was more to it than that. "If he won't behave I don't want him around," McGraw told reporters. "I won't put up with behavior like last year's." He also wasn't very impressed with Douglas' 15 victories in 1921. "I can take any one of the young pitchers on the staff last year and make them win that many. That ought to show where Douglas stands on this club."[29]

But the market for Douglas had dwindled over the years. Neither the Dodgers, Cubs, nor Reds would touch him with a ten-foot pole, as they'd already experienced life with Douglas and weren't about to go down that road again.

The Pirates quickly dismissed any desire to acquire Douglas, and the Braves and Phillies gave no indication they were interested either. Only Branch Rickey of the Cardinals was reported to be interested enough in Douglas to keep in touch with the Giants, which was odd, considering Rickey regularly lectured about the evils of alcohol and had a brother who worked as a federal marshal in the prohibition enforcement wing of the U.S. Treasury Department.

Douglas failed to report for spring training because he was unhappy with the terms of his contract. McGraw reported that he had doubled Douglas' salary, but that the terms were contingent on the pitcher's behavior and the number of games he won. Douglas didn't like those conditions and his teammates figured they'd seen the last of "Shufflin' Phil." But he reported to camp on March 23, "looking fitter than ever and in a mood highly repentant," and was reported to be "in as good condition as any other Giant."[30]

Douglas got off to another fast start in 1922, going 6–1 with a nifty 1.57 ERA in his first nine appearances, and continued to impress into the summer. Then things began to fall apart. He suffered through his worst outing of the year on July 18, lasting only 1 2/3 innings against the Cardinals in a 9–8 loss that pulled St. Louis to within a half-game of the first-place Giants. To make matters worse, McGraw criticized him throughout, causing an argument that lasted until McGraw shouted his pitcher down in the club-house after the game.[31]

Douglas recorded his 11th and final win of the year on July 26 with a less-than-stellar performance in which he allowed five runs to the Cards in seven innings in a 10–5 Giants victory. At that point he was 11–3 with an excellent 2.45 ERA and was by far the Giants' best pitcher.

But it was just a matter of time before Douglas finally imploded and that moment occurred on July 30. Douglas took the hill at the Polo Grounds against the sixth-place Pirates looking for his 12th win and trying to help the Giants keep the second-place Cardinals off their back. But Douglas was pounded by the Pirates for five runs in seven innings in a 7–0 whitewash. Combined with St. Louis' 3–2 win over Brooklyn, the Giants' lead was down to a game and a half.

McGraw accosted Douglas after the game. "Where's your bottle hid?" he demanded. Douglas was taken aback; his poor performance had nothing to do with alcohol. "I want to be traded to St. Louis," he replied. St. Louis was the southernmost major league city at the time and was less than 500 miles from Birmingham, Alabama where he made his offseason home. But Douglas was less concerned with being close to home than he was with being as far away from John McGraw as possible. McGraw flatly refused. "You'll play for me or you'll play for nobody."[32]

The spitballer was despondent and badly in need of a drink, so he headed to a friend's apartment, got drunk and passed out. "Shorty" O'Brien was no longer around—McGraw fired him because not only did O'Brien play cards and go to the movies with Douglas, but he drank with him too, and allowed Douglas to "slip the leash" on occasion. Instead McGraw charged Giants coach Jesse Burkett with keeping tabs on Douglas during the season. Burkett did such a good job that Douglas grew to detest him. But Douglas was able to elude Burkett after getting pasted by the Pirates and he ended up on the Upper West Side getting soused.

While Douglas was "sleeping it off," two detectives posing as representatives of Western Union gained entry to the apartment and found the drunk pitcher in bed. They accused him of stealing a watch from a fan at the Polo Grounds, a charge which Douglas denied, and explained they were taking him into custody. When they attempted to remove Douglas from the apartment, he resisted, which prompted the detectives to threaten to "bring their black-jacks into play" if he continued.[33] The detectives took Douglas to the 135th Street police station, where he was met by Burkett, who then transported the pitcher to the West End Sanitarium, where he was held against his will for five days.[34]

Douglas underwent a grueling detoxification process that included hot baths, stomach pumping and multiple injections of a sedative. Later on, the pitcher insisted he was kidnapped, that as many as five detectives were involved, that his clothes were taken from him and that they refused to allow him to call his wife. Burkett called her to let her know that her husband was alright and McGraw eventually called her to let her know where Douglas was located so she could see him. "I was in bad shape then, and they promised to let me out of the sanitarium on that day," Douglas later recounted. "Instead of letting me go they gave me some knockout drops again and I didn't come to until the following day."[35]

He was eventually released on Saturday, August 5. Ironically, Douglas' disappearance was reported in that morning's newspapers with an interesting claim that "no one could account for his absence."[36] The following Monday he appeared at the Polo Grounds for the first time in a week. Not only was he still under the influence of the depressants he'd been given, but he had spent the previous two days drinking heavily and was barely coherent. When he picked up his mail he found a bill for the taxi ride to the sanitarium and the five-day stay, which amounted to $224.30.[37] When he

tried to protest to McGraw, the manager lit into him and fined him
$100 plus five days' pay (about $188).

According to witnesses, it was the "most vicious tongue-lashing"
McGraw had ever given a player.[38] "He called me the most vile
names...I'll never forget the way he talked to me on that day in the
clubhouse," Douglas later recalled.[39]

That set into motion a series of convoluted events that would
end Douglas' major league career. According to Douglas, when he
learned of the fine, the loss of wages, and the bill from the sanitarium, he also believed he'd been dismissed from the Giants. Already
broke, fearing that he wouldn't be able to make a living, and upset
with McGraw for giving him a "rotten deal," Douglas sat down in
the Polo Grounds clubhouse and penned a letter to Cardinals outfielder Les Mann, a former teammate with the Cubs.

Dear Leslie,

*I want to leave here but I want some inducement. I don't want
this guy to win the pennant, and I feel if I stay here I will win
it for him. You know how I can pitch and win. So you see the
fellows, and if you want to, send a man over here with the goods
and I will leave for home on next train. Send him to my house
so nobody will know and send him at night. I am living at 145
Wadsworth Avenue, Apartment 1R. Nobody will ever know. I
will go down to fishing camp and stay there. I am asking you this
way so there cannot be any trouble to anyone. Call me up if you
are sending a man. Wadsworth 3210, and if I am not there, just
tell Mrs. Douglas. Do this right away. Let me know. Regards to
all. Phil Douglas[39]*

Sending a letter like that was a terrible mistake, especially with
Commissioner Kenesaw Mountain Landis looking to crack down
on crooked players in the wake of the 1919 Black Sox scandal.

But sending it to Mann proved to be Douglas' ultimate undoing. According to author David Pietrusza, "Mann enjoyed a reputation as one of the game's more upstanding individuals."[40] Douglas realized his mistake almost immediately, phoned Mann in Boston where the Cardinals were playing and asked him to destroy the letter. Living up to his stand-up reputation, Mann instead showed the letter to Branch Rickey, who recommended he forward it to Landis.

From there, things spiraled out of control for Douglas. He accosted sportswriter Fred Lieb in the press box at the Polo Grounds following the Giants' 7–3 loss to the Reds on August 8 and told him never to write anything about him ever again.[41] After he calmed down, he admitted that he'd been fined for breaking training and that he was in Burkett's custody. He was also under team physician William Bender's care. Bender went to Douglas' house on Saturday, August 12 and injected him with a depressant. He repeated the injections on Sunday and Monday. Douglas and Burkett left for Pittsburgh on Monday night, where the Giants were to begin a three-game series with the Pirates on Tuesday, August 15.[42]

Landis was also on his way to Pittsburgh. On the morning of August 16, McGraw and Landis met in Landis' suite at the Hotel Schenley, and summoned Douglas for questioning. Landis asked him about the letter, Douglas confessed, and he was immediately placed on the Giants' list of permanent ineligible players and stricken from the hotel register as a member of the team.

When reporters showed up for the impromptu press conference, Landis was "grief-stricken...and looked weary and depressed," and called the incident "tragic and deplorable."[43] When it was McGraw's turn to speak he held nothing back. "[Douglas] admits the charge, and now he is a disgraced ball player, just as crooked as the players who 'threw' the 1919 world's series. He will never play another game in organized baseball, and not a league will knowingly admit him to its parks."

"Personally I am heartily glad to be rid of him," McGraw continued. "Without exception he is the dirtiest ball player I have ever seen and his value to the club has been little or nothing."[44]

It was a ridiculous statement on almost every level. Douglas had much value to the Giants and it could be argued that he was the most valuable pitcher in all of baseball that year. And calling him the "dirtiest ball player I have ever seen" is preposterous considering McGraw managed notorious game-fixers Hal Chase and Heinie Zimmerman, and men like Bennie Kauff, Buck Herzog, Rube Benton, Jean Dubuc, Fred Merkle, and Gene Paulette, all of whom were linked at one time or another to game-fixing, gamblers, or the Black Sox scandal, and some to all three.

Douglas went home to New York and spilled his guts to the press. Soon more details began to come to light, although some were slow in coming. Mann denied any involvement in the scandal, which led reporters to speculate that the Pirates, Cubs, Cardinals, or Reds were involved.[45] But they were ruled out when Douglas repeatedly fingered Mann as the letter's recipient.

Douglas insisted that he was innocent, then muddied the waters even further by claiming he was approached first by gamblers who wanted to fix the pennant race, and he had a letter to prove it. Apparently he figured if he wasn't the instigator, he'd receive leniency. McGraw made things even murkier when he reported that Douglas had been negotiating his "fishing trip" with an unnamed player since January and that the Giants had evidence of such in the form of letters and phone records. McGraw even claimed at one point that he overheard phone conversations between the conspirators, and that he had had his eye on Douglas since opening day.[46]

"I never threw a game in my life," Douglas insisted. "I want the public to know that I am not guilty of any crooked baseball."[47] Douglas' wife averred that Phil was the victim of a "frameup" and that family and friends were conducting their own investigation. Theories held that Douglas was double crossed by gamblers who convinced him to write the letter to Mann, then exposed him to authorities knowing that he'd be blacklisted, which would weaken the Giants and impact the pennant race.

Landis wasn't buying any of it and was convinced that Douglas made the overture to abandon the Giants out of revenge for being "abused and mistreated" by McGraw. He also took one last parting shot at the pitcher. "As for Douglas he is more ignorant than anything else—a foolish, simple fellow who is unmoral rather than immoral. He is amazingly credulous and is inexperienced in many sides of human nature—an easy dupe for others."[48]

Harry Williams wrote, "It is hardly the act of a sane and sober man to put a thing that like in writing...Was Douglas, drunk, the mere dupe of smarter men?"[49] Grantland Rice thought not. "He has not the intellectual capacity for conceiving and carrying through the intricate plans of such men," he insisted.[50]

Mann again refused to admit that he was the recipient of the letter, but flatly denied that a telephone conversation had ever taken place between the two and insisted that he had "never in his life" spoken on the phone with Douglas.

Douglas hired Edward Lauterbach, one of the most popular attorneys in New York, who wasted little time and requested a hearing with Landis. Lauterbach quashed the rumors that Douglas had been a pawn in a larger conspiracy hatched by gamblers, insisting the pitcher acted alone but was not in his right mind when he penned the letter, and that he was under the influence of as many as 20 injections of depressants administered to him.[51]

The Washington Post called the whole fiasco a "dime novel tragedy, involving all allegations of a drunken orgy, a raid, a taxicab kidnapping by detectives, a race to a police station, imprisonment in a sanitarium, a threat to use blackjacks, the use of hypodermic needles, and finally the expulsion of the former Giant pitcher from baseball."[52]

On August 22, it was reported that Lauterbach was prepared to file a civil suit against the Giants for $100,000 if Landis refused a hearing.[53] The Post put the figure closer to $300,000 and quoted Lauterbach as saying, "we may also prosecute on a charge of kidnaping [sic] and false arrest" if Douglas was denied his right to a hearing.[54] A day later, Lauterbach announced that he had obtained "important" affidavits from people who witnessed Douglas' kidnapping by detectives, and from sources who could prove that Douglas indeed made a phone call to Boston and asked that the letter be destroyed, which contradicted Mann's earlier denials.[55]

While Lauterbach awaited Landis' reply to his request for a hearing, the plot thickened. Apparently Douglas told his attorney that he'd been offered $15,000 to throw the games he was scheduled to pitch against the Yankees in the 1921 World Series, but he had destroyed the letter and had no way to prove it.[56] Interestingly, Yankees hurler Carl Mays was under suspicion for throwing games during the same Series, made all the more intriguing by the fact that all three games he pitched were against none other than "Shufflin' Phil" Douglas, two of which he lost, Games 4 and 7, in the late innings under suspicious circumstances. Had gamblers employed a backup plan in the event that Douglas refused their offer?

Landis acknowledged receipt of Lauterbach's request for a hearing, but claimed the attorney failed to produce evidence sufficient enough to reopen the case.

The commissioner's decision, combined with the weight of the case, proved to be too much for Douglas who suffered a nervous breakdown and had to be confined to his Washington Heights

Ben Cantwell

But for a two-year stretch from 1932–1933, Ben Cantwell was as unlucky as they came. During an 11-year career spent mostly with the Boston Braves, Cantwell went 76–108 for a winning percentage of .413. He went 20–10 in 1933, making him the only modern day hurler with a career winning percentage that low to win 20 games in a season (minimum 1,500 innings).

But it was all downhill from there. Cantwell developed bone spurs in his right elbow, but rather than undergo season-ending surgery, he decided to power through the pain. He went 5–11 in 1934, then suffered through one of the worst seasons in big league history when he went 4–25 in 1935 for a Braves team that won only 38 games. To this day the team's .248 winning percentage is the worst in franchise history and it's not even close.

In Cantwell's defense, he received little to no run support during the season—the Braves plated only 3.76 runs per game, by far the worst in all of baseball, and Cantwell got only 2.42 runs of support on average. Compare that to teammate Fred Frankhouse who received almost 5 runs of support per outing and it's easy to see how Frankhouse won 11 of the team's games.

Cantwell won his first start on April 20, but lost his next 13 decisions to fall to 1–13. He sandwiched wins two and three around a 5–0 loss in late July, then lost five more decisions before recording his fourth and final win on August 28. From September 1 until his last appearance on September 27, Cantwell lost his final six decisions to finish at 4–25.

Had Cantwell received just average run support he would have gone a much less embarrassing 13–16. Instead he became the last major league pitcher to lose 25 games in a season.

home.[57] Yearning to return to the south, Douglas eventually gave up his fight, dismissed his lawyer and, with his wife and two daughters in tow, returned to Birmingham.

Things looked like they might turn around for Douglas in 1923 when it was reported that he was being courted by an outlaw team out of Hornell, New York that paid as much as $4,000 for top talent. The Hornell team was allegedly the strongest outlaw team in the country. But players and teams who competed against Hornell were black-listed.[58]

That proved to be a problem almost everywhere Douglas landed. When he signed a deal in early August to play for the Forest City club of the Blue Ridge league in North Carolina, league officials were concerned that other players' eligibility would be endangered. Regardless, Forest City signed Douglas to a contract that was to pay him $75 a week. His stint with the team lasted all of three innings.

Douglas' first and only start came against Caroleen, Forest City's chief rival. The team's management did a fantastic job spreading the news that a former major league pitcher would be suiting up for the club and scores of people from neighboring towns descended on the ballpark.

Douglas allowed seven runs in three innings and the same fans who came to cheer him on, turned on him and accused him of "laying down."[59] That was to be his only appearance. Few realized just how far Douglas had fallen. Making little money to begin with and saving none of it, Douglas lost his Birmingham house when it was repossessed that autumn.

Six months later, in March 1924, Douglas visited the sports department at the Chicago Tribune and announced that Landis had reinstated him and that he would be leaving for Winter Haven, Florida to begin training with the Chicago White Sox.[60] Landis denied the report.

Though it appears things didn't turn out well for him in Forest City, Douglas' semi-pro pitching performances were, more often than not, dominant. He reportedly pitched a handful of no-hitters and one-hitters in places like Pikeville and Tracy City, Tennessee; Lynch, Kentucky; and Bluefield, West Virginia.

Douglas' name appeared again in the papers in December 1925 when the New York Times reported that the pitcher was suing a Pittsburgh sportswriter named Joe Ward for libel for an article he wrote for Baseball Magazine the previous January. Douglas was seeking $100,000, but it's not immediately clear why he filed suit. Ward, a writer for the Pittsburgh Chronicle-Telegram, met Douglas in an all-night restaurant in a seedy part of the Steel City.

When Ward arrived for the interview, the former pitcher was drunk. He described Douglas as "30 years old, looking fifty, his head bowed in grief...He mumbled something we could not understand, but we held our tongue."[61]

Out of pity, Ward bought Douglas a drink and the hurler recounted the events of 1922; how he didn't realize what he was doing, how he tried to have the letter intercepted before it reached Mann. He expressed through tears how badly he wanted to get back into baseball and out of the slums, and how booze was slowly killing him.

"He was a mere shadow of his former self," Ward concluded. "All he had left were the broad shoulders, long and angular now, the strong muscles worn away by the drink. His old familiar shuffle is still there, but it is more like that of an aged man than of the onetime star pitcher. His hair has turned gray and his cheek bones stick out beneath a pair of blazing eyes, the face of a starving man."[62]

After that Douglas shuffled back to obscurity, although he would earn a mention every now and then. In 1927 his wife Louise died of cancer. Her death drove Phil deeper into the bottle—he'd sometimes drink for a week at a time—but even at 38, he continued to dominate semi-pro competition.

He remarried in 1928 and his drinking subsided. He and his family moved from Tennessee town to Tennessee town. Like most residents of Sequatchie Valley during the Depression Era, Douglas was poor. He applied to Landis for reinstatement in 1936, but Landis denied his application.[63]

Douglas eventually landed on his feet working as a foreman for a state highway crew in Jasper, Tennessee, just a few miles from his home. He worked for the Tennessee State Highway Department for eight years until 1949 when a lawnmower blade cut his foot. The cut itself wasn't debilitating, but a blood clot formed soon after, and he suffered a stroke. Unable to work, he lost his job and settled back into poverty, living with his wife in an old log cabin in Sequatchie, paid for by his meager state pension.

He suffered a second stroke in 1951, then a third in July 1952. Down to the last day of his life, he insisted he'd been framed and that his actions of 1922 were not intentional. He died on August 1, 1952 at the age of 62.

In 1990, friends and relatives petitioned Commissioner Fay Vincent to overturn Landis' decision and lift the ban on Douglas on the basis that Landis wasn't fully aware of the reasons Douglas wrote the letter, most notably that he was under the influence of drugs forced on him in during a "brutal" alcoholic rehabilitation program, and that he had an overwhelming hatred of John McGraw.[64]

Unable to recreate the events of 70 years prior and unwilling to second-guess Landis' decision, Vincent rejected the appeal.[65]

PART IV

AMONG THE STARS

"The Kid" Becomes 'Grata' Again

On December 10, 1984 the New York Mets appeared to be on the positive side of a deal that brought All-Star catcher Gary Carter from the Montreal Expos in exchange for infielder Hubie Brooks, catcher Mike Fitzgerald, outfielder Herm Winningham, and pitching prospect Floyd Youmans. At the time of the trade, Carter was considered the game's premier backstop, having supplanted future Hall of Famer Johnny Bench for that honor. He was movie-star handsome, outgoing, enthusiastic, athletic and popular with fans and media. A three-sport star in high school, Carter signed a letter of intent to play football at UCLA before signing with the Expos to begin his professional baseball career instead.[1]

In his 11 years with the Expos, Carter was named to the National League All-Star team seven times, and was twice named MVP of the All-Star Game. He finished second in Rookie of the Year balloting in 1975, and earned MVP votes in all but one year from 1979 to 1984.

Despite his impressive resume Carter's tenure with Montreal had reached a crossroads following a disappointing 1984 season in which the Expos finished fifth in the National League East with a 78–83 record. It was Montreal's worst showing since 1978 and Carter took much of the blame despite enjoying one of his best seasons. It wasn't what happened on the field that rankled Expos management as much as what was going on behind closed doors. Rumors of a divided clubhouse went public. "There has been talk of clubhouse intrigue, racial animosity, petty jealousy, and second-citizen syndrome (double taxation from the U.S. and Canada) for Expo players," wrote the *Street & Smith's 1985 Baseball Yearbook.*[2]

Carter appeared to be in the middle of most, if not all, of it. He was baseball's highest paid player (annually), hauling down $2 million a season after signing an eight-year deal with the Expos in 1982.

When contract negotiations dragged on longer than many had hoped, Expos center fielder Andre Dawson warned that prolonged negotiations could cause dissension among Carter's teammates.[3]

"From what I understand, he's asking for $2 million," Dawson said. "I hate to say that's ridiculous but that's what it boils down to. Personally, I feel that if he wants that much, the team won't sign him. And if we're not going to sign him, we should get something for him while we can and not be like some teams who have lost free agents and gotten nothing."[4]

But the Expos *did* sign him. On February 11, 1982 it was reported that the backstop agreed to an eight-year deal that would pay him an estimated $15 million. Carter refused to go into detail about the pact, except to say it "compares favorably with those of Mike Schmidt and Dave Winfield."[5] In fact, it was Winfield's 10-year, $23 million deal with the Yankees that served as Carter's benchmark during negotiations.[6]

Murray Chass reported the deal was for seven years and called for $14 million and that Carter had received a $2 million signing bonus. The contract also called for incentive bonuses for games caught, awards won, and attendance at Olympic Stadium, which had the potential to make the deal worth as much as $17 million.[7] Thomas Boswell called Carter's contract signing, "...the latest trickle of ice water to chill the game's spine."[8]

Expos president John McHale explained the contract was an extension of the deal Carter signed in 1978 that paid him $115,000 for the first three years and $125,000 over the final two. He also signed a five-year promotional services contract worth $85,000 a year, putting his total salary in the $200,000 a year range.

"We look back at four great years Carter has given us at a salary well below the market," McHale explained, "so we see this as dividing the package by 12 years." McHale justified the contract by comparing Carter's defense to Hall of Famer Roy Campanella and his offense to Bench.[9]

But the March 6 edition of *The Sporting News* painted a picture that was more Edvard Munch than Norman Rockwell. McHale refused to pose for pictures after the signing. "I'm happy that Carter is an Expos player forever and I'm certainly happy that this business is over with," McHale said, "but I'm not in the mood to celebrate." Later, McHale explained "The reason that I couldn't jump up and down with excitement is the system. The price for this kind of contract defies any kind of business logic."[10]

From their inception in 1969 to 1974 when Carter made his big league debut, the Expos' season high in victories was 79 and they never finished higher than fourth. After a cup of coffee in '74, Carter joined the team for good in 1975 and spent most of his time in right field while also serving as catcher Barry Foote's back-up. He hit .270 with 17 homers and 68 RBIs and finished second in Rookie of the Year voting. The Expos went 75–87 and finished in fifth place in the National League East.

Carter suffered through a sophomore slump in his second season, made worse by a fractured thumb that required surgery. He batted only .219 with six homers and 38 RBIs in 91 games in 1976 while splitting time between catcher and right field again, and the Expos finished at a major league worst 55–107.

Carter was named Montreal's starting catcher in 1977 and the 23-year-old responded with his best season to date, belting 31 home runs, driving in 84, and hitting .284. Buoyed by the addition of several new players, including Dawson, who was named the National League's top rookie, and veteran first baseman Tony Perez, the Expos improved to 75–87, but finished 26 games behind the first-place Phillies. Montreal rewarded Carter for his fine performance by signing him to a five-year deal. By all accounts, Carter was thrilled with the deal and hoped to make a permanent home in Montreal.[11]

His up-and-down career slid south in 1978 when his slugging percentage dropped more than 100 points, but he hit 20 homers,

Les Nunamaker

Les Nunamaker.

Les Nunamaker (left) enjoyed a 12-year career with the Red Sox, Yankees, Browns and Indians, and once threw out 51% of would-be basestealers. But his most impressive feat came on August 3, 1914 when, as a member of the Yankees, the backstop picked off Hugh High at second base, then tossed out two potential base thieves to become the first catcher of the 20th century to record three assists in an inning.

Apparently 1914 was a big year for Nunamaker, who hit the only two home runs of his career that season. According to Tony Bunting's biography of Nunamaker, the catcher, who was playing for the Indians in 1920, got a scare when he found a roll of bills under his pillow after Cleveland's Game 5 win over Brooklyn in the World Series.

"Skittish over the breaking Black Sox scandal and taking no chances," wrote Bunting, "[Nunamaker] turned the money over to [American League President] Ban Johnson, who counted the stash." The roll comprised nothing more than 16 Confederate dollar bills, which gave newspapers plenty of comedy material at Nunamaker's expense.[1]

scored 76 runs and drove in 72 to help lead the Expos to a 76–86 record and fourth-place finish. He rebounded in 1979 to hit .283 with 22 homers and 75 runs batted in, was named to his second All-Star team and received MVP support. More importantly, the Expos stunned everyone when they went 95–65 under manager

Dick Williams and finished only two games behind the eventual World Champion Pittsburgh Pirates.

That began a six-year run in which Carter was named to the NL All-Star team each year, finished among the top 20 in MVP balloting in every year but 1983, and won three Gold Gloves. The Expos benefited as well, finishing over .500 for five straight seasons, before falling below that mark in 1984. Carter belted 29 homers and drove in a career-high 101 runs in 1980 and finished behind only Mike Schmidt in MVP voting. Montreal went 90–72 and finished only a game behind the Phillies, who would go on to defeat the Kansas City Royals in the World Series.

During the 1981 offseason, Dick Williams insisted that Carter was the best catcher in the game.[12] Johnny Bench echoed Williams' sentiments[13] and Pete Donovan of the *Los Angeles Times* predicted Carter would be named the NL MVP.[14] Carter felt such high praise should be accompanied by more money.

"I love the Expos and they've treated me fine," he told reporter Milton Richman. "But I'll be 27 in a few days and if I'm being looked on as the best catcher in baseball, it's only natural for me to associate that with my salary."[15] Carter was not only making much less than catchers Darrell Porter and Ted Simmons, but he was making less than most of the players on Montreal's active roster.

In a season split into halves by the first midseason strike in major league history, the Expos won the NL East's second half division title and finished with the East's second best record behind the Cardinals who were shut out of the postseason despite finishing with a division-leading .578 winning percentage. Because St. Louis won neither half of the season, Philadelphia and Montreal battled for the right to play in the NLCS. The Cincinnati Reds suffered the same fate. They finished with the best winning percentage in baseball, but took second place in both halves, leaving the door open for the Los Angeles Dodgers and Houston Astros.

Montreal took the five-game series with the Phillies, three games to two, while the Dodgers defeated the Astros by the same margin, setting up an Expos/Dodgers NLCS. The series kicked off at Dodger Stadium with a 5–1 Los Angeles win, then, to add insult to injury, a French-language daily newspaper in Montreal called *La Presse* reported prior to Game 2 that Carter had rejected an offer from the Expos that would have paid him $1.3 million a year for eight years and that he wanted to play for the Dodgers. Carter denied the rumors, claiming he and the Expos had agreed not to discuss his contract until the offseason.[16]

The Expos won the next two contests and needed to win only one more game to advance to their first World Series. But Los Angeles took Game 4, setting up a memorable Game 5 showdown that went down to the wire. The Expos scored a run in the bottom of the first to take a 1–0 lead over southpaw Fernando Valenzuela before the Dodgers retaliated with a run of their own in the fifth to knot the game at one apiece.

With the score still tied at 1–1 in the top of the ninth, Montreal manager Jim Fanning, who had replaced Williams mid-way through the second half of the season, removed starter Ray Burris from the game. Rather than rely on a bullpen that had been battered by the Dodgers in two of the first four games, Fanning brought in staff ace Steve Rogers. Rogers retired the first two batters, but surrendered a solo homer to Dodgers outfielder Rick Monday and, for all intents and purposes, the game and series were over. It would be the closest the Expos would ever come to the Fall Classic.

The playoff loss was hardly Carter's fault as he hit .429 in 10 games vs. the Phillies and Dodgers with two homers and six RBIs. But that didn't stop trade rumors from circulating only a day after Los Angeles wrapped up its World Series victory over the Yankees. The *Hartford Courant* reported that Carter would be dealt to the Yankees for catcher Rick Cerone, who had traded obscenities with Yankee owner George Steinbrenner during the ALCS after Steinbrenner criticized Cerone's performance.[17]

Ross Newhan reported in late October that the Dodgers couldn't wait to pursue Carter after he became a free agent following the 1982 season.[18] Meanwhile the Yankees were attempting to acquire players that would allow them to offer Montreal more than just Cerone. The plan was to sign Red Sox second baseman Jerry Remy, who was expected to file for free agency, to a contract, then offer Montreal a package that included Cerone, incumbent second baseman Willie Randolph, and minor league pitcher Brian Ryder.[19]

Carter, however, remained optimistic that he and the Expos could reach an agreement on a new deal prior to the 1982 season. In early December, McHale admitted he was "encouraged" by the negotiations.[20] Three weeks later, McHale reported that negotiations had ended and that Carter was weighing Montreal's offer. When asked how he'd come to his $2 million a year asking price, Carter responded, "The standard was set by Dave Winfield...What is Dave Winfield worth to the Yankees? What is Gary Carter worth to the Expos?"[21]

The Expos offered Carter $2 million a year and he finally signed on the dotted line. If there was resentment among his teammates it wasn't immediately obvious. "If anybody is jealous of Gary Carter and his colossal contract, it doesn't show," wrote Joe Falls in March 1982. "His teammates walk by. They look over and grin. 'Way to go Knox', they call out. He looks back and grins. That's what they call him now—Knox, as in Ft. Knox."[22]

But there was resentment among a few members of the media, who were incredulous that a hitter with a career .265 batting average could command so much money. The *Christian Science Monitor's* Melvin Maddocks compared the salaries of Carter, Winfield and Schmidt to those of the Boston Symphony Orchestra's conductor and the president of Harvard, both of whom earned just over $300,000 combined. "Do we really think that money makes Gary Carter ten times as interesting as the conductor of the Boston Symphony?" he asked.[23]

Fans were a bit resentful as well. Booing at enemy stadiums was louder than normal, especially at Shea Stadium in New York, which was ironic considering Mets fans reserved their loudest ovations for slugger George Foster who had recently landed a lucrative deal of his own. Carter responded by enjoying his best season ever, finishing with a .293 average, 29 homers and 97 RBIs and reaching base at a career-best .381 clip. Apparently the fans' attitude towards Carter softened as the season progressed—he was the top vote-getter in All-Star balloting, receiving almost 2.8 million votes.

Carter's numbers tailed off a bit in 1983 but the fans continued to support him in All-Star voting, making him the highest vote-getter among National Leaguers for the second straight season. Expos fans turned on him not long after, though. So did team management. Montreal was only a game-and-a-half out of first place going into September and Carter had just enjoyed his best month of the season, hitting .337 with five homers and 20 RBIs in 26 games. Carter's bat had cooled off over the latter part of August, however, and he hadn't homered since August 17, a span of 19 games and 69 at-bats. He wasn't hitting in the clutch and he wasn't hitting well with runners in scoring position. He was being booed in Montreal.

Despite Carter's troubles, Montreal was on Philadelphia's heels in early September. Carter homered twice in a 10–9 win over the Mets on September 10 to break his long ball drought and propelled the Expos into first place. But they couldn't maintain their momentum and Montreal finished in third place, eight games behind the Phillies. Carter didn't help his cause when he immediately suffered another power outage, failing to homer in his final 21 games. From August 18 to October 2, Carter homered only twice in his last 145 at-bats and finished the campaign with only 17. It was his lowest non-strike year total since 1976.

A few weeks before the season ended, Expos owner Charles Bronfman went on a radio talk show in Montreal and said that it was a mistake to sign Carter to such a lucrative deal and that he was sorry he'd agreed to it. "Two months before Carter signed the contract, we were perfectly aware we were making a mistake," said Bronfman. "The next day, and a month later, we still knew we were wrong. I'll know it until my dying day."[24]

Carter dismissed Bronfman's remarks and insisted he wanted to remain with the Expos. "I think the owner was frustrated and he came down on me," Carter told the *New York Times*. "I feel that I'm part of the reason why we didn't win. I tried my best but I didn't have a Gary Carter year. I just have to handle it in a dignified way. I'll have to come back and make them eat their words."[25]

As winter approached, rumors of a trade with the Cubs began to surface. Amid the trade rumors, there were reports of a "cancer" in the Montreal clubhouse and, though no names were mentioned, Carter felt the reports were directed at him.[26]

His relationship with the press cooled considerably and he announced in March 1984 that he would speak to reporters only after games.[27] His stance was quite a turnaround for someone George Vescey once called "a hyper-version of Steve Garvey, with fewer three-piece suits."[28]

"Both players see baseball as a seven-digit-a-year profession that includes kissing a few babies, shaking a few hands and posing for a few amateur photographers," Vescey wrote. "Depth is not the issue; image is."[29]

Expos management made a handful of offseason moves, one of which brought 43-year-old Pete Rose to Montreal to platoon at first base and in left field. On the surface it was a perfect marriage—Rose had nowhere else to go and by signing him to a two-year deal the

Expos were all but guaranteed of having him in a Montreal uniform when he finally broke Ty Cobb's hit record. But the signing proved to be anything but perfect.

Rose batted only .259 with an anemic .295 slugging percentage in 95 games before he was traded to the Reds in mid-August. He also proved to be a divisive force in the clubhouse, adding to the tension that already existed. Carter accused Rose of caring only about Cobb's record and that he didn't bring the leadership to the Expos that was expected of him. Rose accused the Expos of fostering a losing attitude and said Carter didn't have the "right approach to the game" and that he needed to grow up.[30]

Carter rebounded from his sub-par 1983 season and batted a career high .294 with 27 home runs and a career-best 106 RBIs. He was named to the All-Star team, won his third silver slugger award and finished 14th in MVP voting. Except for the Rose/Carter exchanges, Autumn was relatively quiet and there were no rumors to stoke the flames of the hot stove league. Instead, the Expos simply traded Carter without fanfare. On December 10, Montreal sent Carter to the Mets for infielder Hubie Brooks, catcher Mike Fitzgerald, outfielder Herm Winningham, and pitching prospect Floyd Youmans.

Of the players the Expos received, Brooks was the only established member of the bunch. He finished third in Rookie of the Year balloting in 1981, raising hopes among Mets management (and fans) that they'd finally found someone to fill the vacuum at third base that had existed since the team's inception in 1962.

Brooks broke out in 1984, hitting .283 with 16 homers and 73 RBIs, but he was a below-average third baseman and the Mets were planning on moving him to shortstop before they dealt him to Montreal. Fitzgerald was never much of a hitter and his arm was weak and erratic, especially compared to Carter's, but he earned praise for his ability to call games.

Winningham showed promise in the minors, stealing 50 bases for Single-A Lynchburg in 1982, then hitting .354 in Double-A in 1983 before being called up to Triple-A Tidewater. He hit .281 for Tidewater in 1984, then batted .407 in 14 games with the Mets after a late-season call-up.

Youmans was perhaps the most promising of the four, though. He was only 20 years old at the time of the trade and had not only been a former high school teammate of Dwight Gooden, but was considered as good as, if not better than, Doc. Youmans used a fast-ball clocked in the low 90s to dominate hitters, but he had trouble controlling it, which resulted in high walk totals.

The *New York Times'* Joe Durso reported that the trade had been in the works for 14 months, but it wasn't until new Expos general manager Murray Cook asked for permission to trade Carter in an effort to shake up the club that talks got serious.[31] The Mets were thrilled with the deal, especially since they went into the offseason looking for a right-handed power hitter and a catcher. Filling both holes with one player was a bonus. Carter was equally excited to be going to the Mets. He waived his veto rights as a 10-and-5 player because he felt his addition to an already solid nucleus would lead the Mets to a World Series title. Besides that, he was tired of being blamed for the ills that plagued the Expos. Carter met with Cook in late November and suggested that perhaps it was time for him to move on and that if Cook wanted to trade him, he wouldn't object (Carter had a no-trade clause in his contract that prevented him from being dealt to the Dodgers, Braves, or Angels).

The Mets refused to part with Brooks until they were able to acquire another third baseman. They sent pitcher Walt Terrell to the Tigers for Howard Johnson on December 7, and three days later the Carter deal was made official.

Most cited the obvious; that the trade strengthened the Mets and put them among the National League's elite. They had already taken a giant step in 1984 under new manager Davey Johnson

Gary Carter felt distinctly more appreciated in New York
than in Montreal.

when they won 90 games and finished in second place, 6 1/2 games
behind the Cubs. Maury Allen predicted a two-team race in the NL
East in 1985, giving the Cubs the edge over the Mets, and he picked
the Expos to finish third. About Carter, Allen wrote, "The big bucks
and his teammates' jealousies at Montreal made him persona non
grata. With New York, he is grata, the guy who is supposed to lead
them to October festivities."[32]

McHale couldn't wait to see how the Expos would respond to the
loss of their superstar catcher. "Now we will see what kind of stuff
this club is made of. They won't have Gary Carter to kick around
any more."[33]

The Mets improved by eight games over their 1984 record, going
98–64, but the Cardinals improved by 17 wins, going 101–61, and

finished three games ahead of New York. The Expos finished third as Allen predicted, while the Cubs fell to fourth. Carter acclimated well to the Big Apple, belting a career-high 32 homers and driving in 100 runs to go along with a .281 average.

Brooks hit .269 with 13 homers and paced the Expos with 100 RBIs, becoming the first NL shortstop to drive in that many since Ernie Banks in 1960. Fitzgerald hit only .207 for Montreal, but received praise from Expos pitchers for his ability to call a good game, something Carter rarely received from Expos hurlers. Even though Carter was no longer an Expo, he was still being "kicked around." Winningham was prematurely thrust into center field and struggled. He vowed to match speedster Tim Raines stolen base for stolen base, but fell 50 short of "Rock's" 70.[34] Youmans was called up from the minors in mid-season to help solidify Montreal's injury-riddled pitching staff and he was fantastic in 14 appearances, going 4–3 with a nifty 2.45 ERA.

Carter's premonition about the Mets' bright future came true in 1986 when he helped them dominate the National League to the tune of a 108–54 record, then led them to a World Series victory over the Boston Red Sox. He hit 24 round-trippers and drove in a team-leading 105 runs, then belted two homers and drove in a team-best nine runs in the seven-game Series against Boston. For his efforts, he placed third in NL MVP balloting.

Meanwhile Montreal fell below .500 in '86 and finished in fourth place. Brooks was enjoying his best season and leading the National League in hitting (.340) and slugging (.569) on August 1 when he tore ligaments in his thumb. He missed the rest of the season and finished at .340 with 14 homers and 58 RBIs. Ironically, Fitzgerald, who was also enjoying his best season (.282/.364/.440), was lost for the season in the same game after a foul tip fractured his right index finger. Winningham lost his starting job to Mitch Webster and batted only .216 in 185 at-bats. Youmans anchored the pitching staff and went 13–12 with a 3.53 ERA and struck out 202 batters in 219 innings. He also walked a league-worst 118 batters.

Carter spent three more seasons with the Mets from 1987 to 1989, but his skills began to fade and he was released following the 1989 season. He signed with the Giants in 1990 and platooned with Terry Kennedy behind the plate; moved on to the Dodgers in 1991 and platooned with Mike Scioscia; then returned to Montreal in 1992 for one last hurrah. He finished his career with a .262 average, 324 home runs, 1,225 RBIs, and 1,025 runs, and was inducted into the Hall of Fame in 2003.

Brooks played for 15 seasons, five of them in Montreal, but never came close to reaching the levels he achieved in 1986. He hit 20 homers in a season twice (1988 and 1990) and drove in as many as 90 runs twice (also '88 and '90). After leaving the Expos via free agency following the 1989 season, he played for the Dodgers, Mets, Angels and Royals and finished his career with a .269 mark, 149 homers, and 824 RBIs.

Fitzgerald spent most of his 10-year career with Montreal, playing for the Expos from 1985 to 1991, but he never became a regular and split time with guys like Jeff Reed, Nelson Santovenia, Jerry Goff, and Gilberto Reyes. He retired in 1993 with a career .235 average, 48 homers and 293 RBIs.

Winningham played for nine seasons and bounced around between Montreal, Cincinnati and Boston, hitting .239 with 19 homers, 147 RBIs, and 105 steals in 868 games. He played a small part in the Reds' 1990 run to a World Series title, hitting .364 in parts of five games.

Youmans' career lasted only five years, having been derailed by injuries and drugs. He was placed on the disabled list multiple times in 1987 with a sore elbow, was slapped with a 60-day suspension in

1988 for "failing to comply with his drug-testing program," then underwent arthroscopic surgery on his pitching shoulder in 1989. He spent four years with Montreal and one with the Phillies, compiling a career record of 30–34 and posting a 3.74 ERA in 94 games.

Fred Clarke for Train Fare?

Hall of Famer Fred Clarke was playing for the Savannah Modocs of the Southern Association in 1894 when he was acquired by the National League's Louisville Colonels under bizarre circumstances.

The Modocs, led by Honest John McCloskey, found themselves stranded in Memphis without the means to pay for their lodging or train fare home. Colonels stock holder Barney Dreyfuss bailed the team out and covered the expenses, but in return he asked for Clarke.

Clarke manned left field for Louisville and Pittsburgh for the next 18 years and became a star, hitting a career best .390 in 1897 and leading the league in a handful of offensive categories between 1894 and 1911. He played sparingly from 1913–1915, giving him 21 years in the majors.

Clarke also served as manager from 1897–1915 and won almost 60% of his games with the Pirates from 1900–1915, leading the team to four pennants and a World Series title. His .596 winning percentage is still tops among Pirates managers, and one of the highest of all time.

Clarke finished his career with 2,678 hits and 1,622 runs as a player, and 1,602 wins as a skipper, and was inducted into the Hall of Fame by the Old Timers Committee in 1945.

The Battle for George Sisler's Soul

In 1910, 17-year-old phenom George Sisler signed a contract with Akron of the Ohio-Pennsylvania League between his junior and senior years of high school. Because he was a minor and had failed to garner his parents' consent, Sisler and his father, Cassius, requested that the contract be declared invalid. Sisler then enrolled at the University of Michigan and began playing ball for the Wolverines. In September 1911, Akron sold Sisler's contract to Columbus of the American Association, assuming they still held his rights. In March 1912, Columbus demanded that Sisler report to spring training, but he refused on the grounds that he was still a minor, that he was attending college, and that his parents still wouldn't consent.

Just as Akron had before it, Columbus placed Sisler on its ineligible list and allowed him to continue his college career. Sisler, who would eventually make his mark in the majors as a hard-hitting, slick-fielding first baseman, was a pitcher in high school and college, and began dominating collegiate batters from the day he set foot on Michigan's baseball diamond.

As fate would have it, Michigan's baseball coach at the time was Branch Rickey, who would become one of baseball's top executives, but would first begin a managerial career with the St. Louis Browns in 1913. While Columbus held Sisler's contract, the talented hurler held Rickey's attention. Columbus sold Sisler's contract to Pittsburgh in August 1912 for $5,000 and on September 1, the National Commission approved the deal. As far as Pirates owner Barney Dreyfuss was concerned Sisler was a Pirate and demanded that George report to the team or else be placed on its ineligible list as well.

Afraid that he would lose the remaining three years of his collegiate eligibility, Sisler conferred with Rickey, who convinced

Detroit judge George B. Codd to serve as the young pitcher's legal adviser. Codd, Sisler, and his father all appealed to the National Commission, asking the committee to grant Sisler his free agency on the basis that the boy was a minor when he signed the original contract, therefore it should be declared illegal.

In December the National Commission assured Codd that Sisler hadn't been associated with professional baseball; that his collegiate eligibility hadn't been compromised, and that Pittsburgh's claim to the player would be "dormant" until Sisler graduated from college, at which time the Commission would make a decision on the matter.

Sisler continued to shine at the collegiate level for the next two years while the issue sat on the National Commission's back burner. Other major league teams began to take notice of the young hurler and with graduation only a year away a new sense of urgency cropped up. Codd contacted the Commission in the spring of 1914 and requested that Sisler be declared a free agent so he could negotiate a contract with whomever he chose.

The National Commission knew its hands were tied. Akron had signed Sisler illegally and had no rights to him, which meant that neither Columbus nor Pittsburgh, both of whom had subsequently purchased the illegal contract, had any rights either. But the Commission also understood that Dreyfuss had incurred expenses to acquire Sisler, most notably the $5,000 he sent to Columbus to procure the player.

National Commision chairman Garry Herrmann, on the advice of then National League president Tom Lynch, suggested a compromise that would allow Sisler to become a free agent, but would give Dreyfuss the exclusive right to sign the Michigan star to a contract if he decided to play professionally. Codd rejected the idea and threatened to sue the Commission if it didn't grant his client free agency with "no strings attached."

George Sisler as a Michigan
Wolverine.

"The time is at hand when this young man should be allowed to make a profit out of his own ability and every day's delay is adding to the damage which he is sustaining by your deprivation of his legal rights," Codd wrote. One of the owners suggested that they act in collusion and refuse to negotiate with Sisler, freezing him out of every city but Pittsburgh, so that Dreyfuss could retain Sisler's services without competition. When it was learned through legal channels that the idea constituted a conspiracy and could open major league baseball up to a massive lawsuit, the Commission thought better of it and wisely decided to grant Sisler's request for free agency.

Sisler thanked the Commission and assured them that he would give Dreyfuss every opportunity to sign him to a contract. The Pirates owner offered the collegiate $700 a month for the 1915 season plus a $1,000 bonus, which came to a total salary of $5,200. Under normal conditions, that probably would have been sufficient to get the young star's name on the dotted line. But a new man had taken over the St. Louis Browns' front office and he was making Sisler a better offer.

Rickey left Michigan in 1913 to manage the Browns and serve as second vice president and secretary of the club. It was his responsibility to line up the country's best talent and Sisler was his primary

target. It didn't hurt that the two had already forged a relationship while at Michigan, and when Rickey offered Sisler a salary
of $2,400 for the season and a $5,000 bonus, making the total deal
worth $7,400, Sisler couldn't refuse. Dreyfuss was incensed and
filed a complaint with the Commission, accusing Rickey of tamper-
ing with Sisler and using his personal relationship with the young
man to procure information regarding Pittsburgh's offer, allowing
the Browns to trump it with a more substantial one.

Immediately upon receiving Dreyfuss' formal complaint,
American League president Ban Johnson suspended Sisler, but
incurred the wrath of the Browns and Codd, who threatened
another lawsuit. "I am not courting damage suits," Johnson wrote
to Herrmann. "If you, as chairman of the Commission, want to
assume the responsibility, I will suspend the player on a direct
order from you and the Pittsburgh charge of bad faith can go to a
hearing."

But the suspension was lifted and Sisler was allowed to make
his major league debut with the Browns on June 28. Because the
dispute involved both leagues, Herrmann was responsible for the
Commission's final decision. It took him a year before he finally
decided to dismiss Dreyfuss' complaint due to a lack of evidence.

About the decision, Harold Seymour wrote, "Dreyfuss was
outraged, and his wrath was fed constantly by the sight of Sisler
developing into a great first baseman and one of the best players
ever. The Pittsburgh owner became the implacable foe of Garry
Herrmann and thenceforward bent every effort to unseat him as
chairman of the National Commission."

Dreyfuss' opposition to Herrmann and the National Commission
continued until it was disbanded in favor of a single commissioner
in 1920. Meanwhile Sisler went on to have a Hall of Fame career,
most of it with the Browns, before retiring after the 1930 season
with a career batting average of .340.

But lest you feel sorry for the Pirates, consider this: two months before Kenesaw Mountain Landis agreed to become baseball's first commissioner, the Pirates "stole" a player out from underneath the Boston Red Sox by purchasing him from a minor league team that had an unofficial working relationship with the Sox. The player was to be returned to Boston when Red Sox manager Ed Barrow felt he was ready for the majors, but instead Portsmouth sold him to Pittsburgh for $10,000.

The player? Pie Traynor.

Cy Seymour: Before the Babe

An argument can be made that Willie Mays was the greatest all-around player in Major League Baseball history. On the other hand, Babe Ruth was a Hall of Fame level pitcher before he became arguably the greatest slugger ever.

But prior to Ruth and Mays, there was Cy Seymour (pictured), who won 61 games as a pitcher before becoming a full-time outfielder in 1901. From 1897–1899, Seymour, a New York Giants southpaw, won 57 games and led the National League in strikeouts (twice), hits per 9 IP (once) and K/9 IP (three times). He also paced the circuit in walks all three years and walked more men than he fanned in his career.

From 1899–1904 Seymour was a very good hitter, batting .316 with a 117 OPS+ in 607 games. Then in 1905, he had a season for the ages and missed winning the triple crown by only one homer. In his third full season with the Cincinnati Reds, Seymour batted .377 with 8 homers and 121 RBIs, and led the league in batting, hits, doubles, triples, RBIs, slugging, OPS, OPS+ and total bases. Teammate Fred Odwell hit his ninth homer of the season in his last at-bat of the campaign and kept Seymour from winning the second triple crown of the modern era.

Seymour played six more seasons and never came close to the numbers he posted in 1905, but he finished his 16-year career with 1,724 hits and a .303 average. Since 1893 only Babe Ruth had more wins AND hits than Seymour, yet Seymour has been lost to the annals of history.

The Explosive Bill Dahlen

Bill Dahlen was one of the best players in the earliest days of organized baseball. In 21 years he amassed almost 1,600 runs, 2,500 hits, 1.250 RBIs and 550 stolen bases. And at shortstop he was well above average in the field. Of the 10 players most similar to Dahlen, seven are in the Hall of Fame, and one (Omar Vizquel) might be some day.

But they didn't call him "Bad Bill' for nothin'. As a player, Dahlen earned 33 ejections from umpires, including a career-high six in 1898, but it wasn't until he became a manager that he took the art to a new level.

In 1910 the Brooklyn skipper was tossed from nine games. In 1911 he bumped it to a league-high 11, then posted another league-high with six in 1912. He finished his managerial career with four more ejections in 1913, giving him 30 in only four years. As a player, Dahlen was tossed on average once every 74 contests, but as a manager, he was thrown out once every 21 games.

One of his most infamous clashes came on April 20, 1912 at the Polo Grounds when he and umpire Cy Rigler got into a fist fight following a game-winning walk-off homer by Giants catcher Chief Meyers. With the score 3–2 in Brooklyn's favor, Meyers blasted a shot down the right field foul line and into the "upper tier" of the grandstand that plated two for a 4–3 come-from-behind win.

Dahlen charged out of his dugout and insisted the ball was foul, but Rigler stood by his decision. According to the New York Times, "The scene which followed the Giants' sudden victory was one of the most pronounced outbursts of rowdyism witnessed at a National League ball park in many years."

Dahlen began shaking his fist in Rigler's face and waving his arms "in a wild rage," and the umpire responded by landing a shot to Dahlen's left eye. It escalated so quickly that Wilson hadn't even

"Bad Bill" Dahlen.

reached second base when the fight started. "Bad Bill" retaliated with a right to Rigler's face, and Rigler landed another blow before the combatants were separated by Brooklyn catcher Tex Erwin. They continued to throw punches over Erwin's shoulders before realizing they were surrounded by fans who'd poured on to the field to get a closer look.

Fortunately players and Pinkerton detectives were able to surround Dahlen and Rigler and escort them to the safety of the clubhouse.

Dahlen was just coming off a three-game suspension for an altercation he'd had with an umpire, so NL President Thomas Lynch fined Dahlen $100 and suspended him for two weeks. Rigler earned a $100 fine but no suspension.

Frank Shellenback's Major Minor League Accomplishments

Thanks to an oversight, pitcher Frank Shellenback had a brilliant career in the minors, mostly in the Pacific Coast League, instead of the majors. On the other hand, that oversight might have saved his career.

Shellenback began his professional career in 1917 at the tender age of 18, then made his major league debut on May 8, 1918 with the Chicago White Sox and earned a win in relief of Eddie Cicotte. He went only 9–12 that year, but had a solid 2.66 ERA. He had a cup of coffee with the White Sox in 1919 but spent most of the year with Minneapolis of the American Association.

When major league baseball banned foreign substances in 1920, Shellenback was property of the Vernon Tigers and wasn't grand-fathered in. Fortunately he was allowed to continue throwing his spitball in the PCL and used it to great advantage. From 1920–1935 (his last real full season), Shellenback won 20 games five times, including a career-high 27 in 1931, and averaged 19 wins a year over 15 full seasons. He finished his minor league career with a stellar record of 316–191.

So how did not being a grandfathered spitballer possibly save Shellenback's career? Among his friends were Chick Gandil and Fred McMullin, and among his acquaintances were Lefty Williams, Buck Weaver and Swede Risberg, all of whom were banned for life for their participation in the Black Sox scandal. Had Shellenback stayed with the Sox in 1919, it's possible he would have been caught up in the scandal and finished his professional career with only 48 wins.

Toad Ramsey

Thomas "Toad" Ramsey was the ace of the 1887 Louisville Colonels of the American Association, going 37–27 with a 3.43 ERA, which was very good in a league whose average was 4.29. He made 65 of the team's 139 appearances, tossed 561 innings, completed 61 of 64 starts, and led the league with 355 strikeouts, 5.7 K's per 9 innings, and a 2.13 K/BB ratio.

"Toad" Ramsey (front row, far left) of the
1887 Louisville Colonels.

On June 23 he fanned 17 Cleveland Blues, an impressive total in itself, made even more impressive by the fact that four strikes were required to record a whiff back then. As of this writing Ramsey is the only player named "Toad" in major league history. The Colonels also boasted Chicken Wolf, Ducky Hemp, Ice Box Chamberlain and Peek-A-Boo Veach.

PART V

AROUND THE DIAMOND

The Original Cliff Lee

While doing research, I ran across a Cleveland outfielder named Cliff Lee (not to be confused with the current lefthanded pitcher of the same name), who toiled in the majors for eight years from 1919 to 1926, but appeared in only 521 games and averaged less than 200 at-bats a season. Lee caught my attention because he had a very good 1922 campaign at the age of 25 while playing for the Phillies (he played for Cleveland later in his career) and followed that up with a solid 1923 season. Those two seasons comprised 44% of his playing time. He never reached 500 at-bats in a season; he batted 400 or more times only once in his career and had more than 300 at-bats in a season only twice. So I started to dig for information to find out why a hitter whose slugging percentage (.540) was higher than all but two National Leaguers (Rogers Hornsby and Ray Grimes) in 1922 couldn't crack a starting lineup.

Lee, a native of Lexington, Nebraska, began his career in the Central Association in 1914 without much fanfare and kicked around the Midwest for a few years, before landing in Portland of the Pacific Coast League early in 1918. Lee was apparently the property of the Cleveland Indians at that point, but the Indians admitted to the National Commission that they would most likely send Lee to the minors and that Portland had established the "strongest moral right to the player" and should be awarded Lee's services. After spending a season in Portland, Lee was drafted by the Pittsburgh Pirates in September of 1918.

The Sporting News gave the first glimpse of Lee's abilities when it wrote that he was "considered high class" and "not only a good catcher, but a clever hitter and a fine all-around performer."

Lee joined the service during World War I, but was out in time to join the Pirates roster in 1919. The 6'1", 175-pounder batted only

.196 in 112 at-bats while backing up Walter Schmidt behind the plate and played sparingly in the outfield where he fielded at a .917 clip.

He was penciled into Pittsburgh's lineup in 1920 as the second string catcher behind Schmidt, but failed to hit again (.237/.275/.316) and was relegated to only 37 games and 75 at-bats. Despite his less-than-stellar performance, Lee was courted by an independent league who offered him a $2,000 bonus and a higher salary than what he'd made with Pittsburgh, but he rejected the offer and stayed with the Pirates.

Despite his loyalty, Lee was released by Pittsburgh on April 8, 1921 and was claimed off waivers by the Phillies, who moved him from behind the plate and put him at first base and in the outfield. The move from Pittsburgh to Philadelphia had a positive impact on Lee's batting—he hit .308 with four homers and 29 RBIs in 286 at-bats—but the shift to first base didn't guarantee a starting job.

First sacker Ed Konetchy was selected off waivers from Brooklyn on July 4 and Lee was sent to right field to fight for a job with eight other players, including Irish Meusel and Casey Stengel. While Lee had been an adequate first baseman, he was a terrible outfielder.

Lee entered the 1922 season as a valuable reserve who could play three positions, but he wasn't expected to break into the Phils outfield of Bevo LeBourveau, Cy Williams, and Curt Walker, all of whom were speedsters who once starred for their college track teams. But, though Williams and Walker were two of the league's better hitters that season, LeBourveau couldn't parlay his wheels into success at the plate or in the field. Lee had served as a fourth outfielder and pinch hitter until May 29 when he was suddenly thrust into a starting role in left field. He went hitless that day and was batting only .189 with a home run and two runs batted in on the season heading into the Phillies' May 30 doubleheader against the Giants at Philadelphia's cozy Baker Bowl. From there the right-handed slugger took off.

Facing right-hander Jesse Barnes in the first game, Lee went 3-for-4 with two doubles, a run, and an RBI and was intentionally walked in the bottom of the ninth. It was in the second game that Lee opened everyone's eyes, however. Facing southpaw Art Nehf, Lee homered twice in five at-bats and drove in five runs, and his first homer of the game, a two-run shot in the first, was one for the ages. Wrote the *Philadelphia Inquirer* about the round-tripper:

"Cliff Lee caught one of Art Nehf's left-handed shoots right on the seams in the first inning and the ball soared high and far into the air then disappeared over the left field wall into Lehigh avenue for the greatest home run ever hit on a Philadelphia baseball field. It was the first time a ball has ever been driven over that brick barrier in left field in a game and when the vast crowd realized that this substitute outfielder had turned a feat which great stars of the past and present have never achieved they gave him rousing recognition when he crossed the plate."

It would take another nine years before another batter would accomplish the feat (Boston's Wally Berger homered off Clise Dudley on May 30, 1931).

From June 1 until the end of the season, Lee hit .328 with 14 homers and 70 RBIs and finished the season at .322 with 17 circuit clouts and 77 runs batted in. Based on today's minimum criteria Lee didn't qualify for any titles, but there were no minimum requirements in the early days of baseball (it was all subjective) and Lee would have been considered one of the NL's top batters in 1922. He finished third in slugging, OPS and home runs, and placed among the top 10 in OPS+ and extra-base hits. Only Hornsby and Williams homered at a better pace than Lee.

But a closer look at his numbers shows why he had a difficult time becoming a regular. Later in his career, newspapers often reported that Lee would get most of his playing time against southpaws, leading one to believe that he was either especially potent against lefties or couldn't hit righties well enough to earn more at-bats against them. But that wasn't necessarily the case. Lee was, in fact, better against southpaws, batting .327 with a .372 on-base average and a slugging percentage of .495 during his career. But he wasn't bad against right-handed pitchers, either, batting .282 with a .324 OBA and a .440 SLG, and from 1921–1923 he batted .297 and slugged .459 against righties.

The problem is in Lee's home/road splits. The Baker Bowl was one of the best places to hit in baseball and may have fattened offensive numbers more than any other park in baseball history. In 1922 the Baker Bowl had a HR factor of 234—107 points higher than the next best home run park in the National League, the Polo Grounds. The Phillies hit 95 homers at home, but only 21 on the road. Lee hit all 17 of his homers at home and batted .388 with an OPS of 1.122. He batted only .227 on the road with an OPS of .602.

Despite Lee's prowess at the plate in 1922, no mention was made of him prior to the 1923 season as all the attention went to Art Fletcher, who'd replaced Kaiser Wilhelm as manager of the Phillies. When Wilhelm departed so did Lee's starting spot in left field. Fletcher gave it to 27-year-old former Texas League star Johnny Mokan, who rewarded Fletcher with a solid campaign in which he hit .313 with 10 homers and 48 RBIs in 1923. Lee outhit and out-slugged Mokan, batting .321 with 11 homers and 47 RBIs in almost 50 fewer at-bats. But Mokan was far superior in the field, display-ing a strong arm that produced 16 assists in only 105 games, while Lee continued to plod along with less than impressive results.

The Sporting News gave another indication as to why Lee may have fallen out of favor with Fletcher, writing about his "usual retiring disposition" and that he wasn't planning on doing any work until spring training began. At 6'1", 175-pounds, it's difficult to imagine Lee getting out of shape, but his work ethic apparently left something to be desired, and the Phillies sold Lee to Cincinnati in mid-June 1924.

Lee fell off the radar again until August when Ford Sawyer listed him among his August All-Stars (great players born in August), putting him in the outfield with Harry Heilmann, Baby Doll Jacobson, and Harry Hooper, pretty heady company for a guy who couldn't even start for the last place Phillies and batted only six times for the fourth place Reds, before being shipped to St. Paul.

Cleveland purchased Lee from St. Paul in October 1924 and again he was expected to be a reserve who could provide punch off the bench. He did just that, batting .322, slugging .491 and driving in 42 runs in only 230 at-bats for an Indians team that finished in sixth place in the American League. Only manager and center fielder Tris Speaker finished the season with a higher OPS+ than Lee, yet most of the right field playing time went to Pat McNulty who was a decent hitter and a superior defensive player.

In 1926 *Lee* batted only .175 in 21 games and was shipped to Newark on September 30, 1926 in a deal that sent infielder Lew Fonseca to Cleveland. And with that, Lee's major league career was over.

He played for Newark until the end of May 1929 when his new manager, Tris Speaker, released him. It was the second time in three years that Speaker had parted company with Lee. In 1930 Lee landed with the Seattle Indians of the Pacific Coast League and batted .296 with only one homer in 233 at-bats. Not even in the minors could Lee break into the starting lineup.

In 1937 the 41-year-old Lee appeared in a tournament sponsored by the *Denver Post* that featured former big league stars such as Rogers Hornsby, Grover Cleveland Alexander, and Sammy Hale, among others.

The trail grows cold from there.

Lee passed away in Denver on August 25, 1980 at the age of 84.

Who, You Ask, is Tiny Bonham?

Ernest "Tiny" Bonham, a native of Ione, California, began his career in 1935 and kicked around with a handful of teams, winning 14 games in 1936 with Akron, before landing in Oakland of the Pacific Coast League in 1937. The right hander became the team's ace, winning 17 games and striking out 190 batters, and tossing a seven-inning no-hitter against Seattle on July 4. He almost duplicated the feat a month later when he allowed only one hit,

"Tiny" Bonham, underrated 1940's Yankees hurler.

an eighth-inning single, to the Los Angeles Angels on August 3. He pitched for the Newark Bears and Kansas City Blues in 1938, and it was in Kansas City that the 6' 2", 215 lb. hurler learned his trademark forkball.

Bonham's contract was purchased by the New York Yankees in September, 1939 but he was released back to Kansas City in late March, 1940. He pitched well for the Blues, earning a spot on the American Association All-Star team, before being recalled by the Yankees in early August to "bolster a crippled Yankee pitching staff." Lefty Gomez was battling a sore arm and Red Ruffing, though still effective at 15–12, was 35 years old and in his 17th year at the big league level.

The Yankees had won four straight World Series titles from 1936–1939, but, upon Bonham's arrival on August 2, New York was 7 1/2 games behind the front-running Detroit Tigers and were in need of pitching help.

Bonham lost his first start to the Boston Red Sox on August 5 but fared well, allowing three earned runs in eight innings in a 4–1 loss. "It was the unfortunate lot of the Blues' graduate to make his bow on a day when the Yankees weren't hitting the size of their neckbands," wrote Dawson.

He lost two of his first three decisions, falling both times to the Red Sox, before reeling off five straight wins, one of which was over Bob Feller and the Indians. He lost to the St. Louis Browns by a 2–1 score on September 15, but finished the season strong with three straight wins, including an 11-inning victory over the Senators on the season's final day. With the rookie's help, the Yankees closed Detroit's gap, but they finished in third place, two games behind the Tigers and a game behind Cleveland. Bonham was stellar in his 12 starts, winning nine of them against only three defeats and posting a microscopic 1.90 ERA, and he walked only 13 batters in 99 1/3 innings.

The *Los Angeles Times* averred that Bonham and Marius Russo, a mid-20s star-in-the-making who debuted with the Yankees in 1939 and went 22–11 in his first two seasons, would form the nucleus of the Yankees pitching staff starting in 1941.

Russo indeed anchored the Yankees staff in '41, leading the team with 27 starts and going 14–10 with a 3.09 ERA, Gomez returned to form, going 15–5, and Ruffing continued to defy his age, winning 15 games as well. But Bonham made only 14 starts, going 9–6 and pacing the rotation with a 2.98 ERA in 126 2/3 innings. In fact, the Yankees used 10 different starting pitchers that season and seemingly relied on a seven-man rotation that also included Spud Chandler, Atley Donald, and Marv Breuer.

A balky back kept Bonham on the shelf from mid-May to late June and forced Yankee manager Joe McCarthy to give his ailing starter as much rest between starts as he could get. Bonham had to wear a back brace when he pitched, but the rest of the staff picked up the slack and paced the junior circuit in fewest runs allowed per game, while finishing second to the White Sox in ERA. The hitters also stepped up, led by a trio of 30-homer sluggers—Joe DiMaggio, Charlie Keller, and Tommy Henrich—and the Yankees reclaimed their place atop the American League with a 101–53 record, finishing 17 games ahead of the runner-up Boston Red Sox.

In the National League the Dodgers squeaked past the Cardinals, who were in first place as late as September 1, and finished with a two game edge over St. Louis on the strength of a 100–54 mark.

The *Christian Science Monitor* gave the Yankees the edge over Brooklyn because of the relative ease with which the Bronx Bombers took the AL pennant. "They are coming up to this series... relaxed and ready...Their invalids have had time to get well and their weary have had time to rest...this month-long release from strain might very well be decisive."

Paul Zimmerman of the *Los Angeles Times* picked the Yankees to win in six games. Few disagreed. New Yorkers were so sure the Yankees would easily dispatch of the Dodgers that R. Parfitt Eaton wrote a letter to the *New York Times* facetiously suggesting that Major League Baseball should cancel the World Series as an act of kindness toward the Dodgers.

The Yankees jumped out to an early lead, defeating the Dodgers 3–2 in Game 1 behind the pitching of Red Ruffing and the batting of Joe Gordon and Bill Dickey, who accounted for two-thirds of New York's hits and all of its runs batted in. The Dodgers evened the series at a game apiece with an identical 3–2 victory in Game 2 as Whit Wyatt outdueled Chandler despite allowing nine hits and five walks.

Russo and Freddie Fitzsimmons locked horns in Game 3, trading goose eggs for the first seven frames before the Yankees plated two in the top of the eighth on singles by Red Rolfe, Henrich, DiMaggio, and Keller to take a 2-0 lead. The Yanks literally knocked Fitzsimmons out of the game when Russo lined a ball off Fitzsimmons' leg and, though Pee Wee Reese was able to field the carom and throw Russo out at first for the final out of the inning, broke Fitzsimmons' kneecap. The Dodgers reached Russo for a run in the bottom of the frame, but that was all they could muster and the Yankees took the contest, 2-1.

Game 4 pitted Donald against Kirby Higbe and neither lasted more than four innings as the Yankees jumped out to a 3-2 lead through the fourth. The Dodgers took the lead in the bottom of the fifth, scoring two runs to go up 4-3, but they couldn't hold on as the Yankees staged a ninth-inning rally that plated four runs in an eventual 7-4 victory. It's this game that will live in infamy thanks to Brooklyn catcher Mickey Owens' passed ball on what should have been the final out of a Dodgers' 4-3 win. But with new life, the Yankees strung three hits and two walks together off Brooklyn reliever Hugh Casey to snatch victory from the jaws of defeat.

With a commanding 3-1 lead in games, McCarthy turned to a healthy and well-rested Bonham in Game 5 and he slammed the door on the Dodgers to help the Yankees cop their fifth championship in six years. He held the Dodgers to one run on four hits and two walks and fanned two in the complete game 3-1 victory and retired 18 of the last 20 batters he faced, allowing only a walk and a single over the final six innings.

Irving Vaughan of the *Chicago Tribune* called Bonham "invincible" and lauded the hurler's stellar performance. "The Dodgers attack was melted down to almost nothing by Ernie Bonham," wrote Vaughan. "Real trouble caught up with the young and burly Yankee right hander only in one spot—the third inning—when a pair of hits accounted for the National Leaguers' only run. From this point to the finish he was a master."

Bonham's success continued in 1942 when he was finally able to pitch a full season for the first time. He went 21–5 with a 2.27 ERA and finished fifth in MVP voting, but lost his only World Series start to the Cardinals, who beat him 4–3 in Game 2. That would prove to be the apex of his career. He continued to enjoy immediate success, winning 15 games in 1943 and posting another 2.27 ERA before losing to the Cardinals in the Fall Classic again. But from 1944 to 1949, he went 49–50 while pitching for the Yankees and Pirates and he was only able to reach 200 innings in a season once due to the chronic back pain that plagued him throughout his career.

He was planning on retiring after the 1949 season, but succumbed to abdominal pain in late August and was admitted to Pittsburgh Presbyterian Hospital on September 8 for an emergency appendectomy. While performing surgery doctors discovered that he had intestinal cancer. Only a week later, on September 15, Bonham died at the age of 36.

He finished his 10-year career with a record of 103–72 and a 3.06 ERA.

Charles Stoneham: The Block from Which Horace was Chipped

Horace Stoneham will always be vilified as the man who abandoned New York and moved his Giants to San Francisco, but his father Charles might have been part of a nefarious plot of his own.

The New York Yankees began sharing the Polo Grounds with the Giants in 1912 and moved in permanently in 1913, but in the fall of 1919 the Giants insisted that the Yankees find a new place to play. Accounts had Charles Stoneham disliking the "tactics of the radical element in the American League," and he served Yankee owners Colonel Jacob Ruppert and Colonel Cap Huston with a peremptory notice to vacate the Polo Grounds after the 1920 season.

Suspicions were aroused and AL president Ban Johnson was pegged as the front man in a conspiracy to force the Colonels out of the league by taking away their playing site. With no place to play and little desire to build a new stadium, the Colonels would surely sell the team.

A diary written by White Sox secretary Harry Grabiner that was discovered in a hole in the wall under the stands of Comiskey Park in 1963 outlined a plot that had Johnson attempting to secure the lease on the Polo Grounds so he could place new owners in the American League. In return for granting him the lease, Johnson would allow Stoneham to not only hand-pick the new Yankee owners, but also the third member of the National Commission, baseball's ruling body at the time.

Johnson denied the charges and swore that he was, in fact, attempting to secure a long-term lease for the Yankees, going so far as to appeal to NL president John Heydler, hoping he could convince the Giants to change their minds. But they refused to budge, citing an animosity towards Colonel Huston, who sent letters from France during the war, criticizing the National League for "laxity in war work."

Giants management vowed that as long as Huston was with the Yankees, a long-term lease would not be in the offing and the Yankees would have to find a new home. Hence the eventual birth of Yankee Stadium, which opened in 1923.

Source Notes

The Mysterious and Tragic Death of Don Wilson   p2

1. "Stars of the '70s." Sports Stars of 1968—Baseball, Spring 1968
2. *Los Angeles Times*, January 6, 1975
3. *Chicago Tribune*, January 6, 1975
4. *Los Angeles Times*, June 6, 1974
5. *New York Times*, March 20, 1968
6. Ibid.
7. Ibid.
8. *Los Angeles Sentinel*, January 16, 1975
9. *Los Angeles Sentinel*, July 27, 1967
10. *The Sporting News*, August 5, 1967
11. *The Sporting News*, November 18, 1967
12. Personal interview with Dick Bosman in September 2010
13. *The Sporting News*, November 18, 1967
14. James and Neyer, *The Neyer/James Guide to Pitchers*, p. 429
15. *The Sporting News*, September 7, 1968
16. *New York Daily News*, June 14, 1969
17. Ibid.
18. *Baltimore Sun*, April 3, 1972
19. Ibid.
20. Ibid.
21. James and Neyer, *The Neyer/James Guide to Pitchers*, p. 429
22. *The Sporting News*, January 2, 1971
23. *Chicago Defender*, September 11, 1971
24. *The Sporting News*, December 4, 1971
25. *Baltimore Sun*, July 29, 1973
26. *Chicago Defender*, August 30, 1973
27. *Chicago Defender*, January 7, 1975
28. *Chicago Defender*, March 12, 1975
29. *The Sporting News*, June 1, 1974
30. *Baseball Digest*, June 1974
31. Ibid.
32. *Los Angeles Times*, September 6, 1974
33. *Hartford Courant*, September 8, 1974
34. *Los Angeles Times*, September 5, 1974
35. *Hartford Courant*, September 8, 1974
36. *New Pittsburgh Courier*, September 14, 1974
37. *New York Times*, January 6, 1975

38. *Los Angeles Times*, January 6, 1975
39. *New York Times*, January 6, 1975
40. Ibid.
41. *Chicago Defender*, January 7, 1975
42. *New York Times*, January 7, 1975
43. Ibid.
44. *Hartford Courant*, January 7, 1975
45. *New York Times*, January 8, 1975
46. *Corpus Christi Times*, January 16, 1975
47. *New York Amsterdam News*, January 18, 1975
48. *Los Angeles Times*, February 6, 1975
49. *Chicago Defender*, March 12, 1975
50. *Baseball Digest*, April 1975

Ray Fisher   p18

1. Boston Globe, April 9, 1921

Austin McHenry   p19

1. Portsmouth Daily Times, November 27, 1922
2. Portsmouth Daily Times, October 2, 1915
3. Ibid.
4. Portsmouth Daily Times, November 29, 1922; McHenry's family also believed that the beaning he suffered in 1916 resulted in the brain tumor that caused his death. An e-mail from his great niece confirms this: "I thought my mom and grandmother said that Austin had been hit in the head by a baseball; therefore, I always thought that is what caused his brain tumor." A long-term study of 2,953 people with 29,859 person-years of follow-up after head injury found little to no correlation between head trauma and brain tumors, however, and if there is an association, it was deemed "extremely small." A separate study conducted in Denmark between 1977-1992 found that "head trauma causes, at most, a small increase in the overall risk of brain tumors during the ensuing 15 years."
5. Christian Science Monitor, June 13, 1918
6. OPS+ figures were taken from www.baseball-reference.com and calculated as such: 100*[OBA/lg OBA + SLG/lg SLG-1] (Adjusted to the player's ballpark(s)).
7. Lee Lowenfish, Branch Rickey: Baseball's Ferocious Gentleman (Lincoln, Nebraska: University of Nebraska Press, 2009), p. 111
8. New York Times, September 7, 1919
9. Massillon Evening Independent, November 22, 1922
10. New York Times, May 24, 1921
11. The Sporting News, January 19, 1922
12. Ibid.

13. New Castle News, December 7, 1922
14. Lowenfish, Branch Rickey, pp. 308-309
15. Kansas City Star, December 17, 1922
16. Portsmouth Daily Times, November 29, 1922
17. Chicago Tribune, August 10, 1922
18. New Castle News, August 31, 1922
19. Portsmouth Daily News, November 27, 1922
20. Chicago Tribune, November 28, 1922
21.

Denny Galehouse   p30

1. Hartford Courant, October 4, 1948
2.

Ed Conwell   p44

1. Portsmouth Daily Times, August 7, 1909
2. Ibid.
3. Portsmouth Daily Times, August 18, 1909
4. Portsmouth Daily Times, March 28, 1911
5. Portsmouth Daily Times, August 23, 1912
6. Ibid.
7. Sporting Life
8. Portsmouth Daily Times, September 24, 1913
9. Portsmouth Daily Times, October 25, 1913
10. Portsmouth Daily Times, November 2, 1914
11. Portsmouth Daily Times, June 23, 1916
12. Portsmouth Daily Times, June 27, 1919
13. Portsmouth Daily Times, May 21, 1921
14. Portsmouth Daily Times, August 25, 1921
15. Portsmouth Daily Times, October 20, 1921
16. Portsmouth Daily Times, May 3, 1926

Harry Lunte   p52

1. Mike Sowell, The Pitch That Killed (Chicago: Ivan R. Dee, 1989), p. 17.
3. Washington Post, August 19, 1920
4. The Sporting News, September 9, 1920
5. Sowell, The Pitch That Killed, p. 198, 235
6. Ibid., p. 239
7. The Sporting News, September 16, 1920
8. Chicago Tribune, March 21, 1921
9. The Sporting News, April 21, 1921
10. Ibid.
11. The Sporting News, May 26, 1921

12. Los Angeles Times, March 24, 1922
13. Chicago Tribune, April 7, 1922
14. Christian Science Monitor, July 24, 1922
15. The Sporting News, March 12, 1925
16. Ibid.

John Paciorek   p61

1. *Washington Post*, October 1, 1989
2. Ibid.
3. *New York Times*, September 30, 1983
4. *St. Louis Post-Dispatch*, April 4, 1993
5. *New York Times*, September 30, 1983
6. *Los Angeles Times*, January 31, 1991
7. *Chicago Tribune*, February 20, 1986
8. *New York Times*, September 30, 1983
9. *St. Louis Post-Dispatch*, April 4, 1993
10. *Chicago Tribune*, February 20, 1986
11. *Los Angeles Times*, January 31, 1991

Larry Yount   p64

1. *Los Angeles Times*, July 26, 1964
2. *Baltimore Sun*, June 30, 2002
3. *Los Angeles Times*, July 16, 1994
4. *St. Louis Post-Dispatch*, March 24, 1992
5. Ibid.
6. *Los Angeles Times*, July 16, 1994
7. Ibid.

Art Shires   p68

1. Los Angeles Times, January 12, 1930
2. Chicago Tribune, August 20, 1928
3. Boston Globe, July 10, 1955
4. Washington Post, August 23, 1928
5.
6. New York Times, March 17, 1933
7. Chicago Defender, December 29, 1928
8. Chicago Tribune, March 29, 1929
9. Los Angeles Times, January 12, 1930
10. Hartford Courant, March 31, 1921
11. Atlanta Constitution, April 3, 1929
12. Washington Post, April 4, 1929
13. Washington Post, April 7, 1929
14. Chicago Tribune, May 16, 1929

15. Chicago Tribune, May 17, 1929
16. Washington Post, May 17, 1929
17. Chicago Tribune, September 14, 1929
18. Ibid.
19. Los Angeles Times, January 12, 1930
20. Chicago Tribune, March 13, 1930
21. Chicago Tribune, December 16, 1951
22. Chicago Tribune, January 3, 1930
23. Los Angeles Times, January 5, 1930
24. Chicago Tribune, January 19, 1930
25. Chicago Tribune, July 15, 1967
26. Ibid.
27. Washington Post, November 29, 1930
28. Washington Post, November 11, 1930
29. Chicago Tribune, November 29, 1930
30. Washington Post, November 29, 1930
31. Chicago Tribune, November 29, 1930
32. New York Times, November 30, 1930
33. Washington Post, December 20, 1930
34. Ibid.
35. Hartford Courant, July 11, 1931
36. Milwaukee Journal, September 28, 1931
37. Boston Globe, January 27, 1932
38. Chicago Tribune, April 23, 1932
39. Washington Post, March 14, 1933
40. Chicago Tribune, August 4, 1932
41. New York Times, March 17, 1933
42. Chicago Tribune, January 25, 1933
43. Chicago Tribune, January 27, 1933
44. New York Times, January 28, 1933
45. Hartford Courant, April 8, 1933
46. New York Times, April 19, 1933
47. Washington Post, April 29, 1933
48. Chicago Tribune, April 20, 1933
49. Hartford Courant, April 29, 1933
50. Washington Post, May 24, 1933
51. Washington Post, May 27, 1933
52. Ibid.
53. Chicago Tribune, June 15, 1933
54. Los Angeles Times, July 3, 1936
55. Chicago Tribune, September 6, 1936
56. Los Angeles Times, November 24, 1936
57. Chicago Tribune, May 22, 1937

58. Chicago Tribune, May 9, 1937
59. Hartford Courant, July 1, 1938
60. Chicago Tribune, May 18, 1948
61. Washington Post, December 8, 1948
62. Ibid.
63. Hartford Courant, December 17, 1948
64. Chicago Tribune, February 1, 1949
65. Los Angeles Times, February 12, 1950
66. Washington Post, February 12, 1950

Phil Douglas   p101

1. Los Angeles Times, May 13, 1913
2. Neyer/James?
3. Chicago Tribune, April 3, 1913
4. Tom Clark, *One Last Round for the Shuffler* (Pomerica Press, 1979), p. 17
5. Ibid., p.23
6. Los Angeles Times, August 21, 1922
7. Los Angeles Times, July 18, 1915
8. Los Angeles Times, March 8, 1916
9. Boston Globe, March 10, 1916
10. Sporting Life, April 21, 1917
11. Ibid.
12. Baseball Magazine, August, 1917
13. Washington Post, January 6, 1918
14.
15.
16. Chicago Tribune, August 22, 1919
17. Atlanta Constitution, August 25, 1919
18. Chicago Tribune, August 28, 1919
19. Washington Post, September 2, 1919
20. New York Times, January 13, 1920
21. Washington Post, January 13, 1920
22. New York Times, July 10, 1920
23. Los Angeles Times, September 16, 1920
24. Ibid.
25. New York Times, July 2, 1921
26.
27.
28. New York Times, February 21, 1922
29. New York Times, March 2, 1922
30. New York Times, March 24, 1922
31. Clark, *One Last Round for the Shuffler,* p. 76
32. *Ibid., p. 79*

33.

34. New York Times, August 19, 1922

35. Ibid.

36. Washington Post, August 5, 1922

37. Boston Globe, August 19, 1922

38. Clark, *One Last Round for the Shuffler, p. 84*

39. *Boston Globe, August 19, 1922*

40. David Pietrusza, *Judge and Jury: The Life and Times of Judge Kenesaw Mountain Landis* (Boulder, Colorado: Taylor Trade Publishing, 2001), p. 245

41. Ibid.

42. Ibid., p. 246

43. New York Times, August 17, 1922

44. Ibid.

45. Chicago Tribune, August 19, 1922

46. Chicago Tribune, August 17, 1922

47. New York Times, August 19, 1922

48. New York Times, August 19, 1922

49. Los Angeles Times, August 21, 1922

50.

51. Atlanta Constitution, August 22, 1922

52. Washington Post, August 22, 1922

53. New York Times, August 22, 1922

54. Washington Post, August 22, 1922

55. New York Times, August 23, 1922

56. New York Times, August 24, 1922

57. New York Times, August 29, 1922

58. Atlanta Constitution, February 4, 1923

59. Washington Post, September 17, 1923

60. Chicago Tribune, March 13, 1924

61. Baseball Magazine, January, 1925

62. Ibid.

63. Clark, *One Last Round for the Shuffler,* p. 138

64. New York Times, April 15, 1990

65. New York Times, June 17, 1990

Gary Carter   p122

1. Los Angeles Times, April 8, 1972

2. Street & Smith's 1985 Baseball Yearbook

3. Chicago Tribune, January 9, 1982

4. The Sporting News, January 30, 1982

5. Ibid.

6. New York Times, December 5, 1981

7. New York Times, February 16, 1982

8. Washington Post, February 14, 1982
9. New York Times, February 16, 1982
10. The Sporting News, March 6, 1982
11. Los Angeles Times, February 24, 1978
12. Los Angeles Times, May 22, 1981
13. Los Angeles Times, April 3, 1981
14. Ibid.
15. Los Angeles Times, April 8, 1981
16. Hartford Courant, October 15, 1981
17. Hartford Courant, October 29, 1981
18. Los Angeles Times, October 30, 1981
19. New York Times, November 5, 1981
20. New York Times, December 5, 1981
21. The Sporting News, January 16, 1982
22. The Sporting News, March 29, 1982
23. Christian Science Monitor, May 24, 1982
24. New York Times, September 27, 1983
25. New York Times, October 4, 1983
26. Hartford Courant, March 4, 1984
27. Ibid.
28. New York Times, December 12, 1984
29. Ibid.
30. Chicago Tribune, December 7, 1984
31. New York Times, December 12, 1984
32.
33.
34.

Les Nunamaker   p125

1. http://sabr.org/bioproj/person/790ea82d

Bibliography

Books

Bouton, Jim, *Ball Four Plus Ball Five*. New York: Stein and Day, 1981

Clark, Tom, *One Last Round for the Shuffler*. Pomerica Press, 1979

Dewey, Donald and Nicholas Acocella, *Total Ballclubs: The Ultimate Book of Baseball Teams*. Wilmington, Delaware: Sport Media Publishing Inc., 2005

Early, Gerald, *"Ain't But A Place": An Anthology of African-American Writings about St. Louis*. St. Louis, Missouri, 1999)

James, Bill and Rob Neyer, *The Neyer/James Guide to Pitchers: An Historical Compendium of Pitching, Pitchers, and Pitches*. New York: Fireside, 2004

Jensen, Chris, *Baseball State by State: Major and Negro League Players, Ballparks, Museums and Historical Sites*. Jefferson, North Carolina: McFarland, 2012

Lowenfish, Lee, *Branch Rickey: Baseball's Ferocious Gentleman*. Lincoln, Nebraska: University of Nebraska Press, 2009

Lynch, Michael T., *Harry Frazee, Ban Johnson and the Feud That Nearly Destroyed the American League.*, Jefferson, North Carolina: McFarland, 2008

Lynch, Michael T., *It Ain't So: A Might Have Been History of the White Sox in 1919 and Beyond*. Jefferson, North Carolina: McFarland, 2009

Pietrusza, David, *Judge and Jury: The Life and Times of Judge Kenesaw Mountain Landis*. Boulder, Colorado: Taylor Trade Publishing, 2001

Seymour, Harold and Dorothy Seymour Mills, *Baseball: The Golden Age*. New York: Oxford University Press, 1989

Sokolove, Michael, *The Ticket Out*. New York: Simon & Schuster, 2004

Sowell, Mike, *The Pitch That Killed*. Chicago: Ivan R. Dee, 1989

Veeck, Bill with Ed Linn, *The Hustler's Handbook*. New York: Fireside, 1965

Magazines

Baseball Digest, Baseball Magazine, SPORTS STARS OF 1968: BASEBALL, Street & Smith's 1985 Baseball Yearbook

Newspapers

Atlanta Constitution, Baltimore Sun, Boston Globe, Chicago Defender, Chicago Tribune, Christian Science Monitor, Corpus Christi Times, Hartford Courant, Kansas City Star, Los Angeles Sentinel, Los Angeles Times, Massillon Evening Independent, Milwaukee Journal, New Castle News, New Pittsburgh Courier, New York Amsterdam News, New York Times, Philadelphia Inquirer, Portsmouth Daily Times, St. Louis Post-Dispatch, Sporting Life, The Sporting News, Washington Post

Websites

Baseball-reference.com, Espn.go.com, Retrosheet.org, Sabr.org, SI.com/vault